VICTORY

The Story Cancer Could Never Tell

Colin Edwards

LUCIDBOOKS

I dedicate this book to my dad, Robby Edwards. I am forever grateful for the way you stood unmoved when life hit you in the face. Your peace, your strength, and your faith have marked my life, and your legacy will live on many years from now!

TABLE OF CONTENTS

THANK YOU

To my mom, Belinda. It's been quite the journey. I'm so thankful for the standard you've set as we all walked through it together. Now the world gets to hear the story. You're a warrior, Mom! I love you!

To my brother, Kyle. I love you, bro! There's nobody else I'd choose to walk with during the long journey. You stood in many moments that no teenager should have to stand in, but your faith didn't fail. The perseverance, humility, and honor that you carry are a standard the world needs to see.

To my wife, Lauren. Thank you doesn't even come close. Your heart to give and your constant love inspires me each and every day. You saw my vision from the start and came alongside me to help make it the best it could be. I love you with all my heart!

To Jenny Gallman. You helped bring this book to life with your constructive criticism, suggestions, and guidance. Thank you for every hour you put into helping me tell this story in the best way possible.

To my friends and family. There are too many of you to name. But so many of you played instrumental roles—both on the journey we all walked and on the journey of telling this story to the world. I am forever grateful.

To Alex Perkins. You designed a compelling, unique, and incredibly significant book cover. I truly believe it will help carry this message even further. Love you, man!

To Lucid Books. Your support, guidance, and encouragement have been absolutely incredible. Thank you for believing in me and in this message.

To the Reader. Thank you for reading this. I pray that God uses this story to awaken your heart to His perspective. The view truly is beautiful.

Chapter One

BLINDSIDED

O ut of nowhere. Talk about being caught off guard. Like a deafening explosion in the middle of my living room, everything went silent, and I could hear nothing but ringing. Like a quarterback dropping back to pass and—boom! Speared from behind. Blindsided. Heard no footsteps. No time to prepare. All I remember is that I was up, and then I was down.

I had been hit from behind before, but never like this. I couldn't get up. It was as if I lay prostrate, pinned to the ground, unable to move. I was paralyzed with fear, crippled by anxiety, stunned with disbelief. It couldn't be true.

It was January 3, and we—my mom, my dad, my brother Kyle, and I—had just gotten home from Kyle's basketball game. We walked in the back door, and as usual, I headed upstairs to my room to get ready for bed. But this time, my dad's voice stopped me before I turned the corner. "Colin, you and Kyle stay down here. We've gotta talk about something." The serious tone of his voice grasped me, and I knew something was wrong. Kyle and I didn't speak a word as we made our way to the couch; the pounding of my heart through my chest was the only sound I heard. What could this be about? We both sat down gently, unsure of what Dad was about to tell us. Dad put his hands together, looked down, and then back up at us. With a soft tone, he began to speak. There was a serious look in his eyes. His voice was gentle and calm, unlike the news he had received earlier that afternoon. "We went to the doctor today and didn't get good news. They found cancer in my colon."

It was a phrase I'll never forget. It wasn't a dream; it was real. He continued, but I hardly heard the rest. All I heard was the word *cancer* and my heart beating out of my chest. It was like a bomb had dropped in the center of the room where we were sitting, echoing into the deepest parts of my mind and body, leaving only paralyzing shrills and a piercing ring. Cancer? My dad has cancer?

The word I prayed would never become reality had burst onto the scene in stunning fashion. In a fraction of a moment, innumerable thoughts surged through my mind, each one circling that six-letter word that changes life forever. Like a struggling swimmer fighting to stay afloat, I gasped for air, but to no avail. Overcome with emotion, I sat there petrified, not hearing a word that followed. It had to be three minutes, maybe four or five. With thoughts flooding my mind, I glanced at my mom's tear-filled eyes and then looked at Kyle as his head hung low and his tears hit the floor. The weight of the moment was heavy. Through my own tear-filled eyes, I looked at my dad and saw a serious look that expressed concern, but I didn't see fear. I saw a look that understood the weight of the moment, but I didn't see fear. I saw the look of a husband, a dad, a pastor, and a teacher who was standing face-to-face with a substantial cancer diagnosis, but I didn't see fear.

No one spoke. If they did, I sure didn't hear them. To this day, I have no recollection of everything Dad said, but I'll never forget the tone of his voice. I don't believe I can adequately describe that tone with words, but if I had to try, I would say it was gentle, soft, genuine, and consumed in grace. There was a sense of calmness and peace. It was authentic; it was love. A few moments went by, and my mind finally began to slow down as I refocused on what Dad was saying. He asked if we had anything we wanted to say or ask, but my brother and I just gave him a side nod. There was more testing that Dad would have to go through, so we didn't know the severity of his diagnosis. But it was still cancer, and I knew cancer was a killer.

In that moment, I looked back over the past 19 years of my life and quickly realized this was a turning point in our life as a family. I had never been more afraid than I was at that moment. I wish I could say that it didn't shake me and that I had complete faith and trust in the Lord. But that would be a total lie. It rocked me. I was petrified, unsure, confused, hurt, weak, and caught completely off guard. Blindsided.

About that time, Mom and Dad both walked over to where Kyle and I were sitting on the couch, took our hands, and began to pray. Mom's tears were still streaming as were ours. As Dad began to pray, there was a tangible shift in the atmosphere. It was a remarkable moment. Just minutes prior, it felt like an explosion had sent shockwaves into the air as he revealed the news. Now, with one prayer, I could feel the air shift in the other direction. In my mind, it played out like a war scene in a movie when, after the debris and smoke settle, the devastation becomes clear. Anxiety seemed to slow down within me. I remember a sense of "We're gonna make it through this" rushing in and working its way into my heart and then into my mind. I wasn't sure how, and I had no idea what it looked like, but I knew that somehow and some way we would make it through—together.

As my dad prayed, my eyes steered away from what was in front of me and began to shift toward a greater reality. Isn't that what prayer does? It acknowledges our total insufficiency and simultaneously the all-sufficiency of Jehovah. In those moments when we feel like we're in the valley and our surroundings are towering over us, prayer begins to shift our perspective. It's the posture we ought to live from. At this moment, it was the only posture we could take.

Dad finished praying and looked us in the eyes. First, with a smile across his face, he reminded us that he loved us. Second, he told us not to be afraid. He told us that when we lay our heads down on our pillows, we were not to worry because the call of God was too great upon us.

Dad walked away, I guess to give us a few moments alone. I could tell that Mom was still struggling as she went to their bedroom with tears still in her eyes. Kyle followed right behind her and headed upstairs to his bedroom to get ready for bed. Still recovering from the initial blow, I sat there trying to process all that had taken place. It was a roller coaster of emotions in a few short minutes as my mind ran feverishly, trying to make sense of what was now reality. However, compared to where I was when Dad told us the news, the Lord had brought me to a much better place.

Dad came back, and it was just the two of us in the room. He seemed relaxed. Me—not so much. I had a sense of peace and understanding and even a slight sense of positivity and optimism that everything was going to be okay, but my heart rate was still through the roof as I battled the what-ifs. Dad must have noticed what was going on because he sat down beside me. It was a moment my dad and I shared that I'll never forget. I didn't know if everything was going to be okay, but he put his hand on my back and comforted me with a smile that assured me we would make it through. Then he looked at me with that same smile and said, "I don't know what's going to happen. But I know God has a calling on your life. Trust Him. He'll take you there." That got the tears rolling again. I had no idea what the coming days and months looked like, but I truly believed what my dad told me. The uncertainty was real, but the certainty was all the more real. All in all, this was the instruction I needed. The course was set, the posture was established; onward was the only way to go. I looked at Dad and assured him that nobody would pray and believe for his healing more than I would.

Finally, I got up off the couch to head upstairs and get ready for bed. The night wasn't over. Little did I know I was seconds away from encountering the Lord in a supernatural way that would not only set the foundation for the journey ahead but change my life forever.

My First Encounter

I turned the corner and headed up the stairs. I wasn't even halfway up when, in the deepest part of my being, I heard the Lord whisper into my spirit. Very gently He said, "You won't be moved." I'll never forget those four words. I knew my Father's voice. In the same way I can recognize my dad's voice in a crowd, I knew without a shadow of a doubt that my heavenly Father had spoken to me. I hadn't even asked Him to speak to me. I wasn't in my closet in worship, and I wasn't on my knees in prayer. I was headed to change my clothes and get in bed when I heard Him. Heaven invaded that stairwell I had walked so many times. I hadn't asked for it, but you'd better believe I welcomed it.

When He spoke, the immediate response in my heart was, "Lord, what do you mean?" As I walked, I waited for Him to continue, but I heard nothing. I was encouraged that God had made such a declaration over me, and it was a pretty good feeling, but I was confused because I felt there was more I needed to know. Those four words—"You won't be moved"—ran through my mind as I climbed each remaining stair and turned the corner into my bedroom. I finally reached my bed and sat down. And then He spoke one more time. I heard the same whisper, the same tone. "Because you're standing on the rock." Wow! Spoken so gently into my spirit, those words consumed me. I didn't know what was to come, but I knew that the God of heaven who spoke creation into being had just spoken to me and assured me that this foundation made me unmovable. Anxiety had gripped me just minutes before, but now the peace that surpasses knowledge had come and calmed me (Phil. 4:7). When I couldn't even move, His presence met me and became my strength. As He spoke, heaven came and supernaturally freed me. I had no idea what the journey looked like. I had no idea if cancer would take my dad's life, but I knew I wasn't alone. And that was enough to keep me going.

I sat there a few moments longer as my mind tried to wrap around all that had happened in such a short time. My mind shifted to Matthew 7 when Jesus was on a mountaintop teaching the multitudes. He said:

> *Therefore whoever hears these sayings of Mine, and does them, I will liken him to a wise man who built his house on the rock: and the rain descended, the floods came, and the winds blew and beat on that house; and it did not fall, for it was* founded on the rock (emphasis added).

—Matt. 7:24–25

When the Lord told me I wouldn't be moved, it wasn't a maybe. It was sure. The rock I stand on isn't a pebble, it isn't questionable, and it isn't light. It was, is, and will forever be unshakable.

- - - - - - - - - - -

As I lay down in bed, I was encouraged. I looked back over the night and could see an image playing out in my mind.

Picture it with me.

I saw myself standing on a large rock in the middle of the ocean. The skies are dark, the sea is white-capping as far as the eye can see. I hear the roar of thunder every five or six seconds, each roar followed by a piercingly loud strike as lightning connects with the water around me. The waves are furiously crashing into the rocks beneath, sending rushing water onto the foundation of the rock and over my feet. The water then makes its way back into the sea where it collides with the next crashing wave and is forced back onto the rock. The water is turbulent, and the sea level seems to be rising with each crashing wave. I look around in every direction, but there is no land in sight. I only see the fierce, unforgiving sea that seems to roar with a vengeance. I stand there panicked, waiting for the wave that will be powerful enough to sweep me off the rock and into the violent sea. There seems to be nowhere to go.

I'm sure many of you reading this have found yourselves in this very place. Here's what happens. In the midst of seemingly impossible situations, when we begin to pray and turn our eyes to the Lord, all of a sudden it's as if we look a second time at the horrid conditions surrounding us. It is very intimidating, even daunting and scary. But as we continue to look toward the Lord, we see that He is gently encouraging us to stand up without fear. He is reminding us that the waves, no matter how scary they may be, aren't powerful enough to sweep us off this rock. They could try all day and night. They could crash harder and harder into the side of the rock, but they will never be able to move it.

The Holy Spirit was teaching me that this rock—the place I was standing—is a secure place. I was still afraid of the what-ifs. Honestly, it seemed crippling. But I had a foundation that was sure. So on this rock I'll take my stance, understanding that from this place, the waves will rush, the winds will blow, the rain will fall, but I won't be moved. The opposition, no matter what it may be, is no match for my foundation. Hallelujah! I have the victory.

Chapter Two

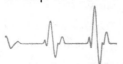

MY SECOND ENCOUNTER

I heard my brother down the hall sniffling through his tears, attempting to come to grips with the same reality I was struggling to understand. I thought about Mom, who hadn't stopped crying since Dad began talking, and my heart broke for her. It was the incomparable love of a mother who wanted to be sure her two sons were okay. It was the unconditional love of a wife who had spent 25 years with this man who was standing face-to-face with the news nobody ever wants to hear.

As I lay my head on my pillow that night, I felt I was in a good place. I knew what the Lord had spoken to my spirit. I knew it wasn't by mistake but rather a timely word that would set the foundation for what was to come. Only He knew what was ahead. Only He knew what I needed for the journey.

He wasn't finished with me yet. I lay there under my comforter with the lights out, peering into the darkness toward the ceiling, never realizing I was moments away from a second encounter with the Lord. On the one hand, I was consumed in the word the Lord had spoken over me, but the what-ifs were still pounding at the door of my very being. As those thoughts flooded my mind, I began to cry aloud again. It was at that very moment, in a way I'd never experienced, a song erupted from me. In the midst of much pain and fear, it rose out of me like a geyser. It wasn't a song that was stuck in my head or a song I had been singing earlier in the day. It was totally random, but it was right on target. I knew it was the Lord.

Words began coming out of my mouth, but even more than that, I began singing them from my spirit. It was a song I had heard many, many times before, but this time it was different.

> Because He lives, I can face tomorrow.
> Because He lives, all fear is gone.
> Because I know He holds the future
> And life is worth the living, just because He lives.

Again.

> Because He lives, I can face tomorrow.
> Because He lives, all fear is gone.
> Because I know, He holds the future
> And life is worth the living, just because He lives.

Once more.

> Because He lives, I can face tomorrow.
> Because He lives, all fear is gone.
> Because I know, He holds the future
> And life is worth the living, just because He lives.[1]

I couldn't shake it. Again. Again. Again. It wasn't soft and shy. It was bold and sure. I have no idea how many times I sang it—20, maybe 25.

---

1. Bill Gaither and Gloria Gaither, "Because He Lives," *MetroLyrics*, http://www.metrolyrics.com/because-he-lives-lyrics-bill-and-gloria-gaither.html.

Each time I sang, heaven was breathing into me; with each word, freedom; with each phrase, strength; with each declaration, hope. It was like a defibrillator that came and shocked life back into me, sending jolts of grace and understanding through my body. I was completely and totally wrecked. Yes, I still stood in the midst of what-ifs. Yes, I still faced uncertainty of the journey ahead. Yes, to some degree, I was still nervous of what could be the final outcome. But in the midst of it all, I received understanding.

Because Jesus lives, I could put my head on the pillow that night and rest assured that my dad would have total victory, regardless of what took place. Because He lives, I could get out of bed in the morning and know that *all* is well, no matter the report. Because He lives, I could continue on, embracing the call of God on my life. At the foundation of my ability to push through and take the next step was the reality that God is alive. Muhammad's body is still in the grave. Buddha is long gone. But Jesus Christ, our Messiah, is alive and will reign forevermore! With that as my assurance, I would take a step. Then I would step again. When it hurt so badly that I didn't know if I'd be able to go forward, I would step again. When doubt was present, I would remind myself of His promise and step again. When I would be at my weakest point, His grace would prove sufficient (2 Cor. 12:9), and I would step. Onward is the only way I would go.

- - - - - - - - - - -

Within the very hour that the enemy unleashed his attack on my family, God taught me something crucial. There was a song in me that had to be released. There was a declaration that had to go forth. Even if my heart or mind didn't understand it, my mouth had to declare it. Even if I didn't feel what I was singing, the declaration reminded me of its truth.

No one else could sing it for me. No one else could praise on my behalf. I had to do it myself.

David wrote:

> *He also brought me up out of a horrible pit,*
> *Out of the miry clay,*
> *And set my feet upon a rock,*
> *And established my steps.*
> *He has put a new song in my mouth—*
> *Praise to our God;*
> *Many will see it and fear,*
> *And will trust in the LORD.*

—Ps. 40:2–3

Initially, I felt like I was drowning, but God brought me up out of that horrible pit, out of the mud, and placed my feet on the rock, on solid ground. Moments later, He put a *song* in my mouth that became my praise to Him.

Trial happens (James 1:2–3). Our response to it is crucial. The question waits to be answered: Will we remain in gloom? Will we fall into depression and embrace the victim mentality?

No, we cannot afford to wait to worship. We must not merely wait until we see the victory come to pass before we worship Him. There's a breakthrough that needs to be sung into existence. There's a freedom and a victory that wait to be released through our praise.

"But," you might say, "this is horrible. The pain seems unbearable. How can I possibly worship?"

I know. Trust me, I know. But here's what it comes down to. God is good—all the time. He's always working on our behalf, and He's taking our miserable situations and turning them into good. So when the news hits, our only and best response is to worship, believing that He is faithful and that He is bringing good out of our circumstance.

In the Old Testament, Moses was supposed to lead the people into the land God had given them, a land "flowing with milk and honey" (Exod. 3:17). However, unbelief (Deut. 1:32) kept them out of this land and confined them to the wilderness where they wandered aimlessly for 40 years. In Deuteronomy 34, Moses's life comes to an end, and God passes the baton to Joshua, appointing him to lead His people across the Jordan River and into the land He had given them. Joshua rose as Israel's courageous leader, fulfilled the command God gave him, and led the people into the Promised Land.

The first place they came to was Jericho, a city fortified against the people of Israel. God, however, had other plans and gave His people instructions on what to do. You probably know the story.

All the men of war were commanded to march once around the city each day for six days. On the seventh day, they were to march around the city seven times, after which the priests would sound their trumpets.

> *It shall come to pass, when they make a long blast with the ram's horn, and when you hear the sound of the trumpet, that all the people shall shout with a great shout; then the wall of the city will fall down flat.*
> —Josh. 6:5

The Israelites obeyed God's commands, and the walls fell—just as God had said.

Here's what we must notice. The shout came *before* the breakthrough. The sound released from the people of God literally gave birth to the miraculous.

Too many of us are waiting to see the victory before we shout. We wait to see the breakthrough before we worship. What if the breakthrough is birthed from our worship?

We want to see our household saved before we release our worship.

We want to see every cancer cell leave before we release our worship.

We want to see the addiction pack up and go before we release our worship.

We want to see depression gone before we release our worship.

We want to see the financial debt eliminated before we release our worship.

We want to see that relationship restored before we release our worship.

We want to see the promotion before we worship the Lord.

Contingent worship is no worship at all. The moment our worship becomes dependent on our circumstance, we've missed it. The moment our worship becomes defined by our life situation, we've missed it. The moment our worship becomes dictated by anything other than His righteousness and our thankfulness, we've missed it.

There's an incredible story in Acts 16 that tells of Paul and Silas being thrown into a Roman prison. While they were locked up, they began *praying and singing hymns to God* during the midnight hour. God sent a massive earthquake that shook the foundations of the prison, broke their chains, and opened the door to their freedom.

In another instance, David was under outrageous distress. The Amalekites raided his city and took captive his family. David's own people were threatening to stone him to death. But he "strengthened himself in the Lord his God" (1 Sam. 30:6). David and his 400 men recovered all that had been taken from them. God preserved them and brought great victory.

A final story tells of a time when King Jehoshaphat received word that enemy armies were converging against him and his people. Immediately, he began to seek the Lord. He proclaimed a fast, and all the people set themselves before the Lord. The Lord spoke to them: "Do not be afraid nor dismayed because of this great multitude, for the battle is not yours, but God's" (2 Chron. 20:15). They positioned themselves for the battle. Some bowed down to the Lord, while others stood up. "With voices loud and high" (2 Chron. 20:19), they worshipped God, who then turned the enemies against themselves. The three armies began to fight each other and then turned on their own. God brought Jehoshaphat a miraculous victory.

It's time we start releasing praise on the front end of the battle that prophesies the breakthrough we'll obtain on the back end. Where is the one who, when faced with an unwanted diagnosis, will shout with victory when it comes? Where is the man of God who will allow trial to thrust him further into the presence of God instead of driving him away? Where is the woman of God who will let worship erupt when all hell seems to be breaking loose in her life? It's not worship that's rooted in fear of what could happen. It's not worship that is pleading with the Lord for a breakthrough. It is a shout that comes from the deepest part of your being, rooted in the promised sovereignty of God and the reality that He's already given the victory. We don't shout for victory; we shout because we already have it!

Victory came by way of the cross. It's already been purchased, and it's already been decided. In covenant with Jesus, we are *victorious*. So may our worship reveal this victory. May our worship, despite the hurt and heartache, sing more loudly than our situation and breathe into every circumstance the victory that He's already purchased.

Hallelujah!

- - - - - - - - - - - -

The two encounters I had with the Lord changed everything. I knew I had a promise. I wasn't going to be moved, no matter how great the storm raged. Upon this promise I took my stance, understanding that because Jesus is alive, I am *more* than a conqueror (Rom. 8:37). From that night on, the Lord began to teach me to live more aware of His presence than the magnitude of my situation. That's what worship does. As I closed my eyes that night to sleep, I didn't know what the future held, but I knew who held it. He's more than enough.

Chapter Three

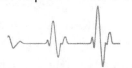

AT FIRST GLANCE

Talk about terrible timing. Dad's cancer diagnosis couldn't have come in a worse season of my life. In every area, I was struggling to find my sense of direction. The previous July, I had moved to Troy University, three hours from home. In high school, I had had a successful basketball career that gave me the opportunity to play at the Division-1 level. During the summer between high school and college, I could not have been more excited. I had dreamed for years of playing college basketball, and it was about to begin. I moved into my dorm and hit the ground running— literally. We began workouts and endurance-building activities, also known as run 'til you puke.

Coach Grant had texted me a few months before I arrived on campus: "Be in shape when you come." I thought I was but quickly found out I had a long way to go. I was 6 feet 6 inches tall and 180 pounds when I graduated from high school. I was too skinny for college athletics and not strong enough to hold my own against other players at my position. They immediately put me on a steady weight-gaining program, which included eating numerous high-calorie meals each day and intense weight lifting three to four days a week.

Preseason came with six weeks of "getting after it," as they liked to say. We had lengthy practices five days a week, with two practices on some days. All that—lifting weights, maintaining my weight program, balancing a full-time academic schedule, and adjusting to new life as a college student three hours away from my family and friends—was no joke.

Before I knew it, November arrived, and the season was less than two weeks away. My body was finally coming along, and I could see great improvement in my strength and agility. One afternoon, I was in the weight room working out like I did any other day. We finished the session with a competitive core exercise and then took to the court to warm up for practice. But something was a little bit off. I experienced a weird pain in my lower abdomen. I went through the next couple of days trying to fight it off, but it progressively got worse. A day or two later at practice, I had a brutally sharp pain in my left hip and groin that ripped through my lower abdomen each time I jumped off my left foot. When I planted with my left foot and cut, I felt the same piercing pain. It didn't hurt when I was just standing, but when it hit, it was real. This wasn't one of those tough-it-out pains. It was a debilitating, stop-you-in-your-tracks kind of pain. Knowing something was wrong, I swallowed my pride and stepped away from practice to visit the trainer.

Over the next month, I was a day-to-day player. Whether I was able to practice or not depended on whether I had any pain when I ran. Ibuprofen and an ice-heat cycle each day didn't do the job. Eventually, I was told there were micro-tears in my abdomen and groin. After a few visits with the athletic doctors, I was given two choices.

1. I could have surgery on my lower abdomen; they would go in and try to find the tears that were causing the pain.
2. I could wait it out six to eight months with no running or weight lifting, let it try to heal on its own, and then see where I stood.

The surgery had a number of risks I wasn't willing to take. So a long waiting period looked like the only answer, but I didn't know whether waiting would even fix the issue. It was going to be a long six months.

To make matters worse, I was struggling to find my sense of direction educationally. I started out as a math education major, but six weeks into Calculus 1, it became very apparent that this was not the route God had for me. I was miserable. I dropped the major and declared "undecided," hoping that clarity would come sooner than later.

Overall, this was a really tough season of life. At first, I was thrilled to play Division-1 basketball, but as time went on, I realized it wasn't quite as great as I thought it would be. It proved to be very grueling, and I could feel the joy I had for playing begin to slowly fade. Now, I was facing an injury that threatened to end my basketball career altogether. Although I wasn't enjoying the game as much, quitting was still a scary thought since I had invested so much time into something that was now on the verge of being taken away. In the moment, it was horrible. I knew people were expecting me to have a successful college career, and that weighed heavily on me. In my heart, I knew it could soon be time to step away. Time would tell.

Christmas break arrived, and because I couldn't run or participate in team activities, my coach let me go home to be with my family. I had not been with them much, so I was thrilled. It was a great upside to a tough situation. But little did I know that toward the end of those two weeks, the news of Dad's diagnosis would come.

- - - - - - - - - - -

The Next Day

After I found out about my dad and after my two life-altering encounters with the Lord, I went to sleep for the night. When I woke up the next morning, it took me a few seconds to remember what had taken place the night before. I hoped it was a dream, but it wasn't. The mental battle was unreal that morning. Although the doctors said it was a big tumor, I knew that Jesus is able. Will He heal my dad? Will this be the end? On the other hand, this was perfect ground for God to come and do the miraculous, but what if God didn't? Cancer has killed many. Would it kill my dad?

All those thoughts surged through my mind in an overwhelming way. I found myself being extremely scared of the unknown. In some ways, I felt like I was subject to the cancer that was in Dad's body, as if I were under its control. I saw cancer as the world sees it. Intimidating. Daunting. Unbeatable. Relentless. Tough. Determined. Unconcerned. I saw its history with the millions of people it has affected. I saw the residue of tragedy and fallout that it left in its tracks each time. I saw the grief, hurt, and agony many families had suffered because of its devastation.

Perhaps that was the issue. Perhaps that was the very reason my mind and heart were spiraling in an uncontrollable whirlwind of hurt. Perhaps that's the reason peace would come and go and not stay. I was never called to see as the world sees. I was called to see from a much higher place—from heaven's perspective.

Too often, we elevate our trials—disease, marital issues, loss, terminal diagnosis, cancer—instead of elevating our perspective. Here's the problem with that. When the trial is elevated, all of a sudden cancer is exalted instead of Jesus, who is Yahweh, Lord of all. Before we know it, we begin to worship cancer with our fear and anxiety, constructing a golden image and laying our hearts down at its altar, begging it to hold back. Through our fear, dread, and anxiety, we give honor to something that is not worthy of honor. The trial that came from the devil only to steal, kill, and destroy is now exalted, even glorified. From that place, our prayers are built on fear when it is the prayer of faith that will make the sick person well (James 5:15). Fear and anxiety run their course, robbing the individual of rest and peace, oftentimes leading to a depressed state. Does this sound familiar to you? The devil is a liar!

Looking face-to-face with a trial is a never-ending cycle of despair. It happens far too often, even in the lives of people who love Jesus. Trial strikes, but the moment we let fear set up camp in our hearts, we've elevated whatever has come against us. Here's the reality. For those of us who are in Christ, we are already positioned in a place of triumph over our enemies (Ps. 27:6 GNT). But when we fear something we have victory over, we take on a new position, stoop to its height, and find ourselves looking straight into the eyes of the adversary. As we look at it eye-to-eye, overwhelming intimidation erupts into more fear and anxiety, causing us to sit back in fear instead of running forward in victory.

David

The people of Israel did the same thing. There was a Philistine giant who stood 9 feet 9 inches tall and carried a sword that weighed 15 pounds. His coat of metal weighed 125 pounds, and he fought in single combat on behalf of his nation. He tauntingly defied the people of Israel and the army of God, demanding that they bring him a challenger. For 40 days, twice each day, Goliath stepped forward and made this request. Each time Goliath spoke, the Israelites were "dismayed and greatly afraid" (1 Sam. 17:11). Each time they saw the champion from Gath, they were "dreadfully afraid" (1 Sam. 17:24).

The people of God looked at the size of their enemy and became consumed by it. They looked out over the Valley of Elah and gave honor to the magnitude of their opposition, spiraling into a place of insurmountable fear.

Let's take a minute and point out that God was with them. It was the same God who separated the waters of the Red Sea to free His people from Egyptian captivity and then engulfed the Egyptian army, killing every last one of them. It was the same God who parted the Jordan River so His people could cross into the Promised Land on dry ground. It was the same God who crumbled Jericho's 13-foot walls, allowing His people to have the victory. It was the same God who took Gideon's 300-man army and absolutely obliterated the 135,000 Midianites. In this story, the people of God were once again standing against adversity, but they were afraid. They weren't looking from the right perspective.

All they could see was a 9-foot-9-inch giant from Gath armed with armor and weapons that were broad and heavy. All they could see was the size of what they were up against and the dreadful defeat that awaited anyone who would confront this giant. All they could see was the track record of the champion from Gath, adding themselves to the list of victims he'd claimed. Now don't get me wrong. He was big and strong. On their own, the people of Israel were no match for such a contender. The problem was that their fear had exalted what was threatening to destroy them, thus elevating their enemy to a place where he looked even more intimidating and even stronger.

In this story in 1 Samuel 17, there was one person who saw differently. He was the youngest of eight boys from the house of Jesse, a shepherd who tended a flock. He wasn't great in stature or build, but he was great in faith. He didn't match up to his older brothers in strength and ability, but he was able to see from a perspective that nobody else was seeing. His name was David, and he was a "man after God's own heart" (1 Sam. 13:14).

While on a mission for his father, Jesse, to deliver food to his older brothers at the campsite, David saw Goliath. He heard the giant's words defying the army of the living God. Wondering why everyone was so afraid, David appeared before King Saul and said, "Your servant will go and fight with this Philistine" (1 Sam. 17:32).

David was looking at the same giant as his fellow Israelites. Goliath had not shrunk in size or become any less in stature or assertiveness. He was still a 9-foot-9-inch champion armed with a 125-pound coat of metal and a 15-pound sword. What changed was that David saw something different. It was as if his eyes were looking through a different lens—a lens of faith. He looked at Goliath and saw how big he was, but even greater than that, he saw how big His

22

God was. He saw the weight of Goliath's armor, but more than that, he saw the faithfulness of God. He saw the size of Goliath's sword, but more than that, he saw the salvation of the Lord. He saw very clearly the opposition, but more than that, he saw opportunity for the glory of God to be revealed. Opportunity to step into divine victory. Opportunity to make known to the nations whose God is the Lord. Hallelujah! As David went to fight the giant with a sling and a stone, God brought the people of Israel a miraculous victory.

Gideon

There was another man 150 years before David who saw from an elevated perspective. Gideon's story in Judges 6 occurred at the time in history when the people of Israel were heavily oppressed by the Midianites. They had been delivered into their hands for seven years as a consequence of their continued disobedience. As the Israelites hid in caves, in the sides of mountains, and anywhere they could find refuge, the Midianites, Amalekites, and the people of the East came and destroyed all their livestock and resources, leaving the people of Israel totally impoverished. In the midst of their anguish and agony, the Israelites called out to the Lord, who responded by anointing a mighty man of valor, Gideon, to raise up the people of Israel and defeat the Midianites. That was quite a task as the Midianites numbered more than 135,000 and would easily annihilate the Israelites who numbered a scarce 32,000. They were drastically outnumbered, and this call to destroy the Midianites didn't make much sense to them. There were 22,000 who quickly stepped away in fear of what could be a devastating end, and that brought the already deficient 32,000 to a mere 10,000.

Twenty-two thousand bowed to fear and yielded. Twenty-two thousand looked straight into the eyes of the enemy and cowered in intimidation. Twenty-two thousand dreaded what could be and gave honor to the very ones who had set themselves up against God and His people. Twenty-two thousand gave their attention to the

Midianite reputation, yielding to their own emotional state instead of to the Lord's call. Twenty-two thousand elevated their opposition instead of elevating their perspective.

Gideon saw differently. He knew the promise of the Lord was trustworthy. He had heard from the Lord, and he believed Him. He saw the same 135,000 men, but more than that, he saw the word of God being fulfilled. He saw the Midianites' track record and their fierce weaponry, but more than that, he saw the deliverance of the people of God. He saw the size of his army, outnumbered 450 times, but more than that, he saw total victory. He saw the freedom of the people of God. He saw the magnitude of the Lord's goodness and faithfulness. He stepped behind enemy lines, fully aware that if God didn't keep His promise, his men were as good as done. His perspective was beyond the 22,000. He saw opportunity for the Lord to be glorified. He saw that by themselves they were no match for the Midianites, but with the Lord, their opposition was no match for them.

Twenty-two thousand stepped away in fear, leaving 10,000 men to fight the large Midianite army. But even this number was more than the Lord needed. After Gideon followed the Lord's leading, the final count was only 300 people that God selected to go fight the 135,000 Midianites.

Three hundred taking on 135,000. I don't have to put that into perspective for you. With natural eyes, it doesn't even make sense. But what took place was remarkable and truly miraculous. The Lord gave Gideon the strategy he needed, and then Gideon made preparations and followed exactly what the Lord told him. The 300 men spread out around the edge of the city and, at the midnight hour, sounded their trumpets all together. They cried out, "The sword of the Lord and of Gideon!" (Judg. 7:18 KJV). The Midianites, awakened from their sleep, were greatly afraid. They were frantic, and in an attempt to flee, they began fighting each other. "The Lord set every man's sword against his companion throughout the whole camp" (Judges 7:22). God brought Gideon and his people a great victory.

There are numerous stories like this throughout scripture. The people of God overcome tremendous odds and arise victorious. It starts when one person who has been with the Lord sees a situation differently. The heartbeat of God is still the same today. In this world, we will have trouble and walk through difficult seasons, but we *must* learn to not stoop to the level of our troubles; we *must* see our opposition from above. We *must* take heart because Jesus has already overcome the world, and through Him, we will do the same.

My Dad

There was another man who saw differently.

My dad had been a lead pastor for 10 years. The morning after his diagnosis, January 4, was a Sunday. That meant he would have to let his congregation know what the doctors had found in his colon. As I was getting ready to go to church, I had no idea what to expect. The five-minute car ride was quiet. We arrived an hour before the service for Sunday school, but I couldn't pay attention to what my youth pastor Ricky was saying. I was still battling the what-ifs, the best- and worst-case scenarios, the many questions that seemed unanswered. The bell rang, signaling the time for everyone to head to the sanctuary for our corporate worship service. We stood to head that way, and everyone entered the sanctuary with smiles on their faces. As I thought about what was about to happen, I couldn't smile. I took my seat in the first row like I always did. I was nervous and antsy, and honestly, I felt a little sick. I didn't know what to expect. As our worship pastor led us in the first song, the congregation stood to join him. After the first song, we sat down for the next two. It seemed like no time went by and worship was over, which meant it was Dad's turn. I looked across the room as my dad stood up and made his way to the stage. I gulped.

I felt as if I were standing on the mountainside overlooking the Valley of Elah, facing the giant of cancer as it taunted me. I was quick to notice its coat of metal and fierce weaponry. I looked and immediately recognized and gave honor to its track record, thus elevating it in my mind. Without realizing it, I lifted my worship toward this giant. I was dreadfully afraid. I felt like I was up against an army 450 times my size, fearful of what the outcome of the battle would be.

My dad asked everyone to open to James 5 as he flipped there in his own Bible. After he read the scripture passage, he looked up and scanned the faces of his congregation. "What do you do when life hits you in the face and turns your world upside down?" He looked around and then asked the question again. As I was fighting back tears, anticipating the news reveal, I quickly peered to my left and then behind me. I saw an unsureness on the faces of the people. They were unsure why he would ask that question.

That's when Dad began to tell the story. Over the next 20 minutes, he shared his heart, and his words blew me away.

My faith isn't in this diagnosis. My faith is in His Word.

Just because someone says something, I'm not going to let it rob me of my life, no matter how short or long I might be here on this earth.

I pray this way, "Lord, the doctor has given me this diagnosis. I give it to You because I don't want to worry about it. I don't want it to burden me. I don't want it to rob me of my Monday. So, I'm going to take it out of my heart; I'm going to lay it down at the altar of God, and I'm going to give it to You. That's my offering to You today! I'm set free of the burden of worrying about what, when, and what if. None of us are guaranteed tomorrow, right? So now I'm free! I'm free to live my life as if I had never heard that diagnosis."

I don't fear cancer, and I don't fear death. Why? I've already overcome through the blood of Jesus.

I preach it, I teach it. Now I get to walk it!

Wide-eyed and inspired, I sat there glued to my dad's every move, locked in to his every word. He was seeing differently. He wasn't looking with eyes of fear but with eyes of faith. Like David and Gideon, my dad wasn't set apart by his stature or his physical strength. It was his faith.

My dad continued:

> When the devil hits me with that fear, you know what I'm going to do? Get out of my life, fear! I'm full of God, His Spirit, and His Word. You can't touch me. There's nothing you can do to me. I'm going to enjoy what I have, whether it's one year or 100 years. Until my last breath, I'm gonna praise Him!

He was looking at the same cancer that we were, but he wasn't intimidated. He wasn't afraid. He wasn't concerned. In one word? He was sure—sure that the palms of the Lord's hands were the greatest place he could be. Sure that no matter what happened over the course of the rest of his life, "Dad is okay."

As Dad began to close his message, he asked the elders of the church to lay their hands on him and pray in faith that the Lord would bring healing to his body. Then he invited everyone who was willing to come forward to encircle the four of us—his family—lay hands on us, and pray. The entire congregation came forward. I was standing to my dad's right, and Kyle was to his left. My mom finished the circle across from Dad. I'll never forget the moment. Dad spread his arms wide, encircled the four of us with his large wingspan, and prayed, "Lord, I place my family in your hands." He then began to praise the Lord.

I was a mess. So were Kyle and Mom. Dad wasn't. He wasn't afraid, worried, or anything remotely close. Dad saw differently. His heart wasn't moved. As we made our way back to our seats, I thought the service was over. But Dad had one more thing in mind. He called the pianist to the stage, and she began playing the old song "This Joy." Dad began to sing, and the Lord knows he can't sing a lick. But he belted it out louder and prouder than ever before, smiling exuberantly with each missed note.

> This joy that I have the world didn't give to me.
> This joy that I have the world didn't give to me.
> This joy that I have the world didn't give to me.
> I'll praise Him all the days of all my life![2]

"How 'bout that. Amen!" he exclaimed, knowing he had messed up the last line of the stanza. Many in the congregation began to laugh and cheer, and I couldn't help but grin ear-to-ear.

Dad wasn't done. "On the second!"

> This peace that I have, the world didn't give to me.
> This peace that I have, the world didn't give to me.
> This peace that I have, the world didn't give to me.
> The world didn't give it and the world can't take it away.

With the help of Blake, our music director, Dad got the last line right this time. His excitement and joy had spread throughout the congregation. It was fun; it was real. He stood front and center and left the people with one sentence. "This is not a sad day. This is the day that God has made, let us rejoice and be glad in it."

- - - - - - - - - - -

No matter how great the opposition may seem and no matter how fierce it may appear, may our first glance not be our last. May the position of our hearts not be based on what we see in the natural but on what we know in the Spirit. May our stance not be influenced by past experience but on the promise of God and the Word of God. May we learn to think and see from an elevated perspective because it's in that place that we are positioned for great victory.

---

2. Shirley Caesar, "This Joy," *eLyrics*, https://www.elyrics.net/read/s/shirley-caesar-lyrics/this-joy-lyrics.html.

Chapter Four

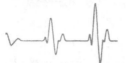

THE SECRET PLACE

When I was a young kid, I used to be afraid of losing Dad. Night after night, I lay in my bed with my eyes wide open, staring up toward the ceiling into the darkness. As a pastor, Dad got calls all the time and would have to leave late at night to go pray with people or go visit someone in the hospital. When the phone rang, I knew it was going to be a long night because I could never go back to sleep until Dad got home. I wanted to be sure he got home safely. As I lay there, bad scenarios ran through my head with each passing minute. It was torment. But now, in this season we had just entered, I was face-to-face with what I had always feared most.

With life circumstances that are ever-changing and unpredictable, people are in desperate need of constancy—a place that won't change. We need an anchor that will hold the ship still while turbulent waves pound all around and chaotic winds tear through the sails. We need a place of security that will remain when all else seems unsure.

That was my heart—desperate, longing, and hungry for a place where I could reside that felt safe. A place I could dwell in the midst of great opposition. A house I could live in that would withstand the fierceness of the storm.

The fight was real.

I felt a pounding in my heart trying to convince me that the emotional unrest and lack of peace were normal. It was as if the enemy were saying to me, "You may as well get used to it because it's the way things have to be." Society tried, too. It seemed as if people around me were trying to use my current stage in life as a way to justify my fear and anxiety. Some would tell me, "It's okay to be afraid." "There's a healthy sense of anxiety." "It's totally normal to be that way." But there was a whisper in my spirit that was urging me to another place. A desperate desire for a place outside of what was accepted as "normal" and "the way things had to be" was being birthed within me. It wasn't a whisper that was passive and timid. It was strong and urgent. There was an ache in my heart that screamed for a new dwelling place in the Spirit. There was an urgency that let me know it needed to happen quickly.

It was the Spirit of God calling me to a secret place, a hiding place, a place behind a closed door (Matt. 6:6). A place beyond the Sunday morning service and Wednesday night life group. A meeting place with the Lord. I read devotionals often, and I read my Bible some nights. I even watched sermons on YouTube during my spare time. But this draw I felt in the deepest part of me was something else—something more. It was the call to a place of vulnerability and sincerity. A place of humility. A place that wasn't casual but intentional. It was a place where I would truly run after the Father's heart with tenacity and zeal. I knew that merely hanging on until the season ended was not the heart of God for me. I knew that Jesus saved me for way more than sitting in hurt and frustration as the season passed by. I knew there was *purpose* for my life, for my family, and for being where we were. But I also knew there was only one place I would discover the purpose.

It was the call to a deeper place. It was as if this new journey was going to require more of me. The Lord was leading me into a place of communion with the Holy Spirit, a place where I could truly yield my heart and give the Lord access to mold and make me into the perfect masterpiece He created me to be. It was the draw to a genuine, wholehearted pursuit of the face of Jesus. A place like the beginning of time. A place in His presence.

The Redemption Story

Access to such a place was established in the very beginning in a place called the Garden of Eden. Adam and Eve were created in perfect harmony with God. The relationship between earthly beings and their Creator was one of unity and peace. It was truly beautiful, free of hindrance and strife. Humanity and God were one!

You may know the story. Tragedy struck in Genesis 3 when man and woman disobeyed God's commandment. In a fraction of a moment, the oneness that God had intended to carry into eternity was lost. God, who is perfect and holy in nature, can have nothing to do with sin. Now that humanity had sinned, God and humanity were separate. No more perfect harmony, no more perfect unity. Only consequence and the righteous judgment of a just God.

In the Old Testament, the Israelites built a tabernacle as a place where the presence of God could reside. Specifically, He dwelled in the inner court, a place called the Holy of Holies, or the Most Holy Place. Only the high priest was allowed to enter on certain terms at certain times. He was the one who stood on behalf of the people and offered sacrifices to God that would *temporarily* atone for their sins. These sacrifices were offered year after year, but they could never totally atone for people's sin and separation from God. The blood of bulls and goats could not take away sins (Heb. 10:4) but only put off the punishment another year.

At the end of the Old Testament, it seemed as if there was no answer. God and humanity would forever be separated. The people had rebelled time and time again, consistently profaning the name of the One who so desperately wanted to restore the relationship.

But then God, in His goodness and mercy, responded with the response of all responses. His only Son stepped off His throne and took on the form of a man. He was heaven's final answer, *Yeshua Hamashiach*, the Anointed One, the One who would do what every man and woman ever born was unable to do. He would fulfill the law once and for all (Matt. 5:17). The Messiah burst onto the scene in extraordinary fashion—Jesus Christ, the Son of the living God.

It was His blood, the blood of the spotless Lamb of God, that would be the propitiation for our sins (1 John 2:2). It took one who was righteous, who was perfect in every way, for us to be made right with God again.

What took place on Calvary was more than a man dying for sinners. It was more than a man paying the punishment that should have been ours. It was more than a false accusation and a wrongful crucifixion. It was God whose heart was totally on the line as He expressed how desperately He wanted to know His people once again. It was the compassionate cry of a God who chose to become flesh so we could see Jesus and see the height, width, and astounding depth of the love of God demonstrated toward us (Rom. 5:8). There was a joy that was set before Him (Heb. 12:2) that far outweighed the agony and hurt of having the sin of the world placed on His flesh. He counted the cost and counted it worthy to restore the relationship between God and humanity.

As Jesus yielded His spirit to the Father, the veil of the Temple tore from the top to the bottom (Matt. 27:51). This monumental, iconic, celebratory moment in history bought back our access into the Most Holy Place, the place where the presence of God resided. Before we even called out to Him, He answered (Isa. 65:24). His answer was Jesus. Once and for all. Done. Complete. Finished.

The place we had access to in the garden, the perfect harmony and unity, free of guilt, shame, and condemnation was reestablished!

The betrayal.

The arrest.

The accusation.

The cursing.

The spitting.

The whipping post.

The Via Dolorosa.

The crown of thorns.

The nails.

The cross.

And Jesus did it *all* just so we could be together again.

- - - - - - - - - - -

Here I was faced with a choice. To sit back, try to get by, and wait for the season to end or to get up in zealous pursuit of the heart of God, believing that His presence was more than enough to carry me through. It was a pivotal turning point in my life. It was as if I were standing at a crossroad looking to the right, then to the left, then back to the right, then back to the left. Which way do I go? To be honest, the pain was so real at times that I didn't want to do anything. Crippling pain, crippling fear, and crippling anxiety would rise up in the deepest part of me. But in my heart, I knew there was only one choice. Despite the pain and confusion, I went after the Lord.

Suddenly, my life launched to cloud nine, and everything was back to normal (just joking). Although part of me wished that had been the case, it couldn't have been further from the truth.

Resistance and opposition set up camp inside me and followed me around everywhere I went. I felt like I was being attacked from every side. I was still going to college, still sidelined with a groin injury, not allowed to participate in any team activities. I was still three hours away from my family during the hardest time we had ever had. My dad still had a massive tumor in his colon.

I began to deal with personal issues in my heart. It was as if an all-out war had been launched on my soul. I quickly found myself in a place of isolation with no accountability. I stumbled into pornography and used it as a way to escape the pain I felt in my heart. It would temporarily sweep the hurt under the rug, but then guilt and shame would bombard me and leave me in a worse place than I was before. My flesh had taken over my spirit. It was a horrid cycle of defeat and guilt. I would fall, feel horrible about it, try to fix it on my own, and then fall again. Looking back, how insane it truly was! I was seeking the Lord—or so I thought.

It didn't make sense to me. I was reading my Bible. I was praying, but nothing improved. In fact, at times it felt as if things got worse. I bought some headphones and listened to worship music on my 10-minute walk to class every morning and then between classes. I thought I was doing it all right, but nothing changed.

I wanted out so badly, but I felt stuck. I was in quicksand. When you step into quicksand, the worst thing you can do is panic and begin to flail around. That will only cause you to sink deeper. That was me—panicked, afraid, flailing. My spirit desperately wanted to be free, but my flesh was in control.

I knew something had to change.

It Begins Within

Perhaps I thought that merely reading the Word of God was an easy out of a tough situation. Perhaps I thought that praying about the day was my one-click fix to a horrible season. Perhaps I thought that if I played worship music, the sound of heaven would be absorbed by osmosis into my heart and mind and my life would turn around and the chaos around me would cease. That was nowhere near the truth.

The problem was that I was seeking the Lord in hopes that the pain would stop. I didn't like the noise and the chaos around me, and I wanted God to fix it. I didn't like the hurt I felt in my heart, and I wanted God to change it. My prayer life revolved completely around my dad's healing and my emotional stability.

I continually prayed, "Lord, please, please, please heal my dad," or "God, you've gotta do something about this." In other words, I was trying to convince the Lord to change the situation around me so the turmoil within me would also change. If the circumstances were all right, I would be all right. But that is not the way. There was an issue in my heart; my focus was misplaced.

It took me months to truly begin to understand. I tried everything. I tried to control my flesh and emotions through willpower and sheer grit, but found I was no match for what I was up against. The more I tried, the more lust, fear, and worry amped up their game. I tried my best to suppress them but only temporarily pushed them away until the circumstances would stimulate them again. I finally got to the place where I realized I couldn't do it on my own. It was in this place of desperation that the Lord began to work in me. He began in my heart.

God is highly interested in saturating the hearts of the ones He loves with His presence and goodness. However, in order for that to take place, I knew something was required of me. I had to go after His heart. Yes, my dad had cancer. But if I sought the Lord merely in hopes that He would heal my dad of cancer, I had missed the point. Yes, I was miserable with college basketball and being away from my family, but if my prayer life was motivated by the hope of feeling better about my situation, I had missed the point. Yes, I made mistakes and was battling guilt and shame, but if my worship was driven by the guilt I felt in my heart, I had missed the point. Then I began to realize something. It was less about me trying to change my actions and more about me pursuing His heart.

Let me explain. The reality is this: If we try to change our actions without also seeking a clean, purified heart, we only eliminate the symptom without going to the source. If we can get our hearts pure, then our actions will follow. The Bible says it this way: "Above all else, guard your heart, for everything you do flows from it" (Prov. 4:23 NIV). It begins in the heart. Always.

So with this new understanding and a second chance, I went after God's heart—not to fix my situation but to learn from Him with hopes of seeing as He sees. As life moved forward, the Lord began to teach me how to pray. I'd pray, "Lord, how do you view this situation? It didn't catch you by surprise." Then, from that place of humility, I postured myself in worship and let Him lead and teach me. I began to dive into the Word of God, desperate to understand His heart. Here's what I discovered. I found that my present sufferings cannot compare to the glory that is going to be revealed (Rom. 8:18). I found that God works *all* things for the good of those who love Him (Rom. 8:28). I found that He keeps in perfect peace those whose minds are stayed on Him (Isa. 26:3).

I'll keep going. I found that His grace is sufficient for me and that His strength is made perfect when I'm at my weakest (2 Cor. 12:9). I found that He is a shield around me and the lifter of my head (Ps. 3:3). I found that His name is a strong tower (Prov. 18:10) and an ever-present help in times of trouble (Ps. 46:1).

As He revealed His heart to me, I began to see more clearly who He really is. Sure, I wished He would take me out of the storm and make it stop, but this time, He was taking me through it. I began to change the way I prayed. Instead of praying about the horribleness of the situation, I asked the Lord to deal with me. I wanted Him to fix me. I wanted Him to teach me how to stand even when I didn't think I could. My prayer became, "Lord, I'm feeling these things in my heart. They aren't in yours, so they ought not be in mine. As best I know how, I surrender these thoughts to You."

Let's look at fear, for example. My prayer became this: "Lord, I'm so afraid right now. But You told me in Your Word that You didn't give me the spirit of fear (2 Tim. 1:7), so I surrender that to You. I thank You that You love me, and that Your perfect love is chasing out any fear" (1 John 4:18).

And then there was my prayer about anxiety. "Lord, I am so anxious about this situation, but You told me not to be anxious about anything. So, as best I know how, I release that anxiety to You, and I thank You that You're covering me in peace that surpasses knowledge" (Phil. 4:7).

And then there was worry. "Lord, I keep finding myself worried about the outcome of this situation. It is keeping me awake at night and consuming my thoughts during the day. You commanded me in Matthew 6 not to worry about tomorrow because tomorrow has enough worries of its own. So I release worry to You. I ask You to come and help me trust You. Always."

Lust. "Lord, my flesh is begging me to appease it. I'm sick of it. I don't want to appease it, but my body is craving it. I'm desperate. As best I know how, I surrender these emotions and these desires to you. I ask you for a pure heart!" Once the emotion rose within me, I prayed it again, again, and again. I prayed that way more times than I can count. But by faith, I believed He was accomplishing my desire, which was also His desire all along. I believed that His grace was making this desire a reality in my heart.

You see, experiencing the emotions of life is a normal thing. The devil's tactic is to shame us for feeling a certain way. Our mistake is attending to those emotions without surrendering them to the Lord. They then become like poison in our hands, robbing us of our today.

As I learned to pray this way, I could feel the shift as He began to anchor my heart in a greater reality. The chaos around me was brutal, but I was becoming more okay as the inward condition of my heart was no longer dictated by the circumstances around me. As the weeks went by, I was beginning to experience a sense of freedom. There was opposition, but my heart and my eyes were set on Him. Transformation was taking place.

Intimacy with the Holy Spirit

It is called intimacy. It is a place in the Lord where I don't run to out of obligation or duty. It's a place I run to in Him and dwell there because it's the place I long to be. It's the place Jesus died so I could have access to Him once again. It's the place where I can just enjoy being with Him!

Looking back, I realize something now that I wish I had realized then. The magnitude of the opposition that seemed to ambush me was actually revealing the value of what I was seeking. Intimacy with the Holy Spirit is where we are called to live and where the enemy most rightfully hates. Why would a thief intrude a house that has nothing valuable in it? He wouldn't. In the moment, I didn't recognize that. I fell into the trap of believing that just doing Christian things was the answer. That is never the answer. John 17:3 says, "And this is eternal life, that they may know You, the only true God, and Jesus Christ whom You have sent." Knowing Him more is the position from which I must live my life.

Intimacy with God takes place when we, as the bride, open ourselves to the bridegroom, Jesus, and give Him total permission to lovingly and gently saturate the deepest part of us with His presence and His loving kindness. David expressed his intimacy with the Lord in profound ways. Here is what he wrote:

> One thing I have desired of the LORD,
> That will I seek:
> That I may dwell in the house of the LORD
> All the days of my life,
> To behold the beauty of the LORD,
> And to inquire in His temple.
>
> —Ps. 27:4

To dwell with the Lord was not the *first* thing David desired. It was the *one* thing He desired. It's truly remarkable. David didn't just want to be with the Lord for a time and then step away and engage in something else. His desire was solely to be with the Lord all the days of his life. He didn't want to wait until heaven to live in a reality he could experience now. His heart was to bless the Lord at all times (Ps. 34:1). His posture was to dwell in a place where He could gaze upon the beauty of the Lord and learn from Him (Ps. 27:4).

Intimacy desires to be. It doesn't strive to perform in order to gain acceptance. It enjoys communion. It enjoys relationship. It enjoys being with someone.

In an era when people have many different beliefs about who God is and what He's all about, the truth is that it was for intimacy that Jesus died. In a society that is incredibly focused on who can be more right, may we never get too analytical that we miss the simplicity of just being with the Lord. May we never get lost in the status quo of engaging in aimless theological disputes rooted in pride, but may we know the heart of God more completely each day. May we never get lost in striving tirelessly to become what God has already declared us to be, but may we always live aware of why we were created—to know God intimately.

- - - - - - - - - - -

As the journey my family was on progressed, I began to recognize that we weren't alone. I got texts from friends who found themselves in similar circumstances. Their questions were the same each time: "What do I do?" I didn't have a long answer, and it wasn't overly spiritual, but it was the only answer I knew to give.

We have *got* to be with God!

Wherever you are right now, take a moment and examine yourself. You may be in a place just like I was. You may feel stuck. You may feel like there's no way out. Be encouraged. The Lord is calling each of us to a quiet place. Whether we are problem-free or all hell has broken loose in our lives, the Spirit of God is drawing us to a place away from the noise of society and to a place of intimacy where we can truly get to know the heart of the Father.

This secret place is where:

- our hearts are molded.
- our minds are renewed.
- our desires are transformed.
- our callings are birthed and realized.
- restoration is found.
- gifts are stirred up and uncovered.
- the peace of God comes to us.

- - - - - - - - - - -

If you are facing difficult circumstances, you have a choice to make. You can either sit back and hope the season passes by quickly or, in the midst of the season, decide to intentionally go after the heart of God. That's when things truly begin to change, when you decide it's going to be more than a get-by devotion time and a check-it-off time of prayer. Instead, you decide to embark on a wholehearted pursuit to know God—to *really* know Him. It begins alone. Shut the door behind you. Seek Him, and you will find Him (Jer. 29:13). It will make all the difference.

The greatest calling on my life is to know the only true God and to know Jesus Christ whom He has sent (John 17:3). I refuse to just look toward the mercy seat and enjoy the view from afar. I'm running in, full speed ahead. Then I'm going to make His presence my dwelling place for the rest of my life. At the end of my life on this earth, that's what I'll stand for—not for how many sermons I preached, how many books I wrote, or even how many people I won to the Lord. I'll answer only to my relationship with Jesus Christ.

So what's my posture moving forward? I'm going after the heart of God. I'm going to truly get to know Him. As I do, by His grace, I will become more like Him. His presence is where I want to be.

Chapter Five

TAKE A WALK

I remember exactly where I was when I got the call. I could take you back to the very parking spot. I was sitting at Troy University behind the dormitory where I lived during my freshman year. I had parked in that particular spot numerous times before, but this time was one I would never forget.

Mom's voice was calm, her demeanor collected. However, I could tell it was a pretend calm. It was one of those moments where you know without any doubt that the news is not good. So you suffer through the small talk, wishing the reason for the call would come up sooner than later. We've all been there.

I knew Dad was having a scan that day to determine the extent of the cancer. How big actually was this thing? Where exactly was it located? If the tumor was high enough in his small intestine, he would have part of his colon removed. Then they would reattach it, and life would go on. That was what I had hoped for at least.

The small talk came to an end, and the moment arrived. I sat anxiously with my heart pounding, desperately hoping that the news was good. But I knew it wasn't.

The scans revealed the worst. Massive in size. Located at the lower end of his colon. As one doctor put it, "This tumor could have been there two or three years." Three or four lesions on the liver. Numerous hot spots in his lymph nodes.

Stage IV.

Mom didn't use that phrase, but she didn't have to. I'm sure she had prepared for the conversation. She didn't water down the reality of where we stood, but she didn't magnify it, either. I recognized her honesty and concern, and I appreciated it. I knew this news also came as a shock to her. She went from life being normal and routine to her husband being hit with a cancer diagnosis, only to discover a few days later that it's stage IV. So, from the get-go, I made a commitment to grab the positive, highlight it, and be her constant encourager.

I was very unfamiliar with cancer. I just knew it was bad and that its track record was pretty brutal. When Mom told me it had spread to the liver and lymph nodes, I thought to myself, "Well, just go in there and take it all out. Let's get on with it!" I quickly found out that it didn't work that way. A stage IV metastatic cancer diagnosis meant it was inoperable. Chemo was the only medical option.

When we finished talking and hung up, I felt like I had the liberty to let it all out. I sat weeping in my car for what had to be an hour. As tears streamed down my face, I began to look back over the past few weeks to when things were so normal. Now, all of a sudden, things weren't. I sat there confused, trying to process everything. I began to look ahead, wondering how the journey was going to look and what the final verdict would be. As I thought about my personal life, I knew it was time to step away from college basketball for good. I wanted to be free to be with my family as often as possible during this journey. A culmination of emotion erupted all at once, but it was the uncertainty of the future that scared me the most. Will Dad die? Will he live? Ultimately, that's all I wanted to know.

News began to spread about the stage IV diagnosis. I received texts from friends, some distant and some close, expressing their deep sympathies as if my dad had just gotten his death sentence. For a 19-year old trying his best to think positively and look at the bright side of the whole situation, their words made it seem like the end of the road was in sight. I didn't like it. I stood face-to-face with the question that everyone in similar circumstances has to face: "What do I do now?"

I had my posture. My stance was established. My foundation was sure. But now, the rains had become torrential, and the winds had strengthened. Let's put it this way. The fire was hot, but it just got hotter. And I asked, "What do I do?"

There were three Hebrew boys in Daniel 3 who also faced a devastating trial. They were Shadrach, Meshach, and Abednego—friends of Daniel. The trumpet sounded, which was everyone's command to bow down to King Nebuchadnezzar's golden image. But these three audacious young men refused, fully aware of the fatal consequences that awaited them in the fiery furnace. At the King's command, they were apprehended and brought forward, given one final chance to bow down. They stood firm in their commitment to God. Nebuchadnezzar's fury raged, and he commanded his men to heat the furnace seven times hotter. Then, they cast the men into the fire.

Let's get one thing straight. This fire was *hot*. It was so hot that it killed the guards who cast Shadrach, Meshach, and Abednego into the furnace (Dan. 3:22). Let's get another thing straight. Shadrach, Meshach, and Abednego were *in* this fire. They weren't looking from a distance, and they weren't just standing close by. They were right smack in the middle of it, completely surrounded by this intense blaze.

As I let this story play out in my mind, I could see myself standing there. I looked around and could see the flames roaring. I could feel the intense heat against my body. The smoke made it hard to breathe. I began to look ahead—weeks, months, even years. I felt like a runner who was five miles into a marathon with more than 20 miles to go. Panting, hurting. The end is a long way away. What do I do?

Look back to the story in Daniel 3.

King Nebuchadnezzar, whose guards were now dead, looked into the fire and was astonished at what he saw. Shadrach, Meshach, and

Abednego were walking around, unhurt. Here's what scripture says: 'Look!' he answered, 'I see four men loose, walking in the midst of the fire; and they are not hurt, and the form of the fourth is like the Son of God' (Dan. 3:25).

The fire, which scholars say was more than 1,000 degrees, didn't burn them. It didn't even debilitate them. And here's the key to it all: They were *walking*.

How is this possible? There was One with them in the fire who was superior to the fire in every way. There was One walking with them whose dominion and authority crushed any power the fire had. He was Jesus, the Son of God.

The same One who was with them in the fire told me He would also be with me: "When you pass through the waters, I will be with you; and through the rivers, they shall not overflow you. When you *walk* through the fire, you shall not be burned. Nor shall the flame scorch you" *(emphasis added)* (Isa. 43:2).

- - - - - - - - - - -

Let's be honest with ourselves. When life gets hard, sometimes all we want to do is lie down and do nothing. Sometimes, all we want to do is sleep, hoping that closing the curtains, turning the lights off, and shutting our eyes for a few hours will help us escape the world around us. We can become so mentally, emotionally, and physically drained during these seasons that we wish we could forget it all. Yes, yes, yes. I've been there many times! In our trials, if we aren't careful, we can become debilitated and chained. How? Well, when we live under the influence of circumstance, we lie down defenseless when in reality we have every weapon we need to win. Before we know it, we are lying there as a victim instead of rising up as a victor.

This story in Daniel paints a life-changing picture. In a trial, the first thing we must understand is that God is with us. If we don't understand that, we're already defeated because the opposition is stronger than we are. The reality that He is with us equips us to rise up out of the pit that was set for us because the opposition is no match for Him. In the case of Shadrach, Meshach, and Abednego, they were equipped to rise up in victory and walk through the furnace that was designed to destroy them. The heart of God for us is the very same—that the trial will not debilitate us but that, in the fire, we will maintain our posture of worship and walk through it, exiting the trial freer than we were before we entered it.

Let's look at this picture another way. I'm going to speak from personal experience. I hate sprinting. Period. Perhaps it's because I had to run sprints so often in high school sports or when I was playing college basketball. Perhaps it was because I was never as fast as the others. I'm not really sure. Regardless, I hate to run sprints. There was always a time limit and a pressure to do it faster the next time. There was always a required speed and a punishment for not being fast enough. Now to the one who loves sprints, more power to you. However, I do enjoy an afternoon jog or a leisurely walk. Sometimes, when I get home from work, I'll change into shorts and a T-shirt, slide on my tennis shoes, and set out on a jog—one mile or two miles, depending on the day. On other days, I'll finish up dinner, let it settle for a little while, and then set out on a casual walk around the neighborhood with no expectations.

I believe this paints an incredible picture in the spiritual realm. As we walk with the Lord, we often feel the overwhelming obligation to perform a certain way. We view it more as a dreaded workout we have to get done than a lifestyle we can enjoy. We carry the heavy weight of expectation, believing the lie that we have to achieve a certain speed or mile marker, which robs us of the joy of leisurely walking with Him through this life. To put it simply, our focus is on performing well rather than enjoying the walk with Him.

I've learned that walking with the Lord isn't an exhausting place; it's a place of extraordinary rest. As I continued to walk, what was exhausting at first actually became enjoyable. The more I walked with Him, the more I could feel the striving and the obligation to perform well lift from me. I learned each day to simply take the Lord by the hand and enjoy our stroll together. Society constantly pounds at our door saying that we must do more. If we aren't careful, social media teaches us that we are never going to live up to what others make themselves appear to be. We feel as if we aren't doing enough. As we seek the Lord, we often sit down and believe that if we didn't read five chapters, we didn't do enough. If we didn't pray for a whole hour at one time, we didn't do enough. But the Holy Spirit isn't saying that. He is drawing us into the place where we learn to abide with Him each day, not merely for a period of time.

I don't want to imply or suggest that it is wrong to set aside time, because it's important. Many times, I've sat down with the Lord to read a certain number of chapters or spend a certain amount of time in prayer. However, it must not be merely about the time so we can check it off for the day. It must not be about performing well and placing an expectation on ourselves that God never placed on us. Sometimes, we can just sit down to read the Word of God, get stuck on one verse, and meditate on it. Sometimes, we can just sit with the Lord in silence and enjoy His presence. Sometimes, we might begin to read and pray and then get so caught up in it that we can't stop. But whatever happens, it's about the joy of being with Him all day every day and walking through this life with Him, learning from Him and becoming like Him with every step. After all, that's why Jesus gave His life—so we could be together again.

Some of you may need to take this literally and go take a leisurely walk. Try it. As you walk, allow the Lord to bring tremendous freedom to you as He reminds you that there's not a certain mile number or top speed you have to attain. He just wants to enjoy the walk with you. Just walk. As you learn to walk and enjoy it, you'll learn to run well. The Christian life is not a sprint; it's a race. Enjoy the journey.

Shadrach, Meshach, and Abednego did that. So in the fire, I'll do the same. I'll keep walking. I'll keep stepping. My walking isn't going to be out of obligation; it's going to be something I greatly look forward to. When I get tired and feel too weak to go on, His strength will meet me, and I'll take another step. If I fall, I'll get back up. When I feel like I can't step again, His grace will prove sufficient, and I'll step once more. I'm not even focused on the end anymore. I'm focused on the journey. I'm going to enjoy it all. With my eyes on Jesus and with our hands together as one, I'll put one foot in front of the other. Step, step, step. That's all I know to do.

Chapter Six

THROUGH THE FIRE

The next 16 months were grueling, full of ups and downs. We faced many disappointments and celebrated many victories. We saw incredible miracles, and we also saw prayers go "unanswered." The blaze was raging, and the fire was hot, but God never left us. He took us by the hand and led us *through the fire.*

January 2015

Ten days after being diagnosed with cancer, Dad began chemotherapy. The doctors who put together a treatment plan were really optimistic. The plan was for Dad to undergo four cycles of aggressive chemotherapy and then have a PET scan, track the progress, and decide on further therapy. Dad would go in twice every other week—Mondays and Wednesdays—and sit for three or four hours each time as the treatment was administered. He also received a pump that he carried with him for the 24-hour period following each treatment. This was such an odd season. So much had quickly transpired, but now it was as if time stood still as we waited and prayed.

It was not an easy road to walk. I was unsure of the future, but I had to keep stepping. I would doubt the outcome, but I had to keep stepping. Each day was another step. Even when I was frustrated because there was nothing I could do to help, I stepped again. Days turned into weeks. Weeks turned into months. Some days I thought the day would never end, but I made it through.

Doubt seemed to be my biggest struggle. I believed that God could work a miracle in Dad's life—that's an obvious thing. But I doubted if He *would*. It wasn't a question of His ability because He's God and really capable. But the war was within. Will He do it? Will He heal my dad? Because you'd better believe I was praying that He would.

Here's where I went wrong. When doubt crept in, it was my tendency to panic because I thought I was outside of faith. I started believing that because I wasn't in faith, God wouldn't perform the miracle I had been praying for. It quickly became a horrible cycle of doubt and shame, which I would counteract with striving to believe harder. I found myself trying to muster up something from within that can't be created but only received. How twisted! I had to learn not to condemn myself for doubting—something that just confirms I'm human. What became crucial was that in the midst of doubt, I had to transfer my attention and begin to pray, recentering my focus on the promises of God. Then I stepped. The intent of doubt is to paralyze and keep the doubter from stepping forward in the Lord. When we recognize doubt for what it is, surrender it to the Lord in prayer, and then *step*, that's when freedom comes. When we step forward in the Lord, pray, and *trust* Him despite what we feel or think, we leave the doubt behind and press forward into the promise of God. I found great peace in the stepping, because the worst thing I could do was linger in the emotions that would hold me back from where God was calling me.

Our First Miracle

April 2015

Dad was three months into chemo, and the progress was unreal. He had a PET scan, and even the doctors were amazed at what the scan revealed. I remember looking at the scans side by side.

The one on the left was the scan from January 2015, and the one on the right was from April 2015. Although I had never seen a PET scan, it didn't take any prior knowledge to see the change. The glowing spot that stood out like a sore thumb in the first was now closer to a small speck. The tumor in his colon, which was initially 10 centimeters, had shrunk to less than half that size. To paint a better picture, it had shrunk from the size of an orange to the size of a pecan. What a day it was! The Lord was doing it. He was healing my dad.

Dad was scheduled to undergo another four cycles of chemotherapy with the hope that it would continue to wipe out the cancer.

May 2015

It was the beginning of May 2015. A lot was happening. Dad had been through another four weeks of chemotherapy and was set to have his second scan to track the progress. My college semester was ending, and my last final exam was scheduled that day. I had already emptied my dorm room, and my car was stuffed full. I was ready to go. This exam was the only thing that separated me from heading home to be with my family for the summer. The exam was in Computer Concepts, and it wasn't going to be easy. Throughout my school career, I had never received anything less than an A. In order to continue the streak and maintain my 4.0 grade point average, I had to make a 94 percent on the exam. For the past two weeks, I had done hardly anything but prep for that final exam. I reworked every example I could find, studied the textbook, studied with friends, and took online sample tests. Anything that would help, I tried.

The time came for the exam, and I arrived at the assigned classroom, which was full of computers. The exam began, and I felt decent about the questions. Of course, there were a few I questioned, but I could at least make an educated guess. There were only a few problems left, and I knew that making 94 percent was going to be close. Real close. Too close.

After checking through my work one final time, I nervously clicked the "submit" button. I was instantly greeted with a big fat 88 right there at the top of my screen. In that moment, the past 12 years of A's rushed through my mind. The moment I had hoped would never come was now a reality. Tears began to stream down my face (okay, totally kidding about that part; that would be a bit dramatic). But it was a little disappointing. Nothing could be done about it now—what's done is done, right? I shrugged it off, gathered my things, and off I went. It was time to go *home*.

I hopped into my car and left. That's when the phone rang. It was Dad. As we talked, I told him about the final exam. He wasn't even a bit concerned. He told me he was proud of me for working hard and doing my best and then quickly shifted the conversation. He had gotten the results of the scan.

"My liver is clear!"

Initial scans had shown several cancerous spots on his liver. This scan showed they were *completely* gone. God was doing it! He was healing my dad. This was huge news! It had only been four months since Dad was diagnosed with stage IV cancer. But now, since the liver was clear, he could have surgery to remove the tumor in his colon. Cancer-free was in sight. I didn't care anymore about the 88 percent. I didn't care about the 4.0. The cancer in my dad's liver was gone! Praise the Lord!

June 2015

After a visit with two surgical teams and his cancer doctor, Dad was set for surgery. He would continue chemotherapy until he finished his scheduled cycle on June 24. The hope was that the chemo would shrink the tumor and allow the surgeon to remove the cancerous segment and reattach his colon. Because the tumor was so low in his rectum, the doctors were concerned that they wouldn't be able to reattach it. If that happened, Dad would have to have a colostomy after the cancerous segment was removed. To put it simply, he would have to poop into a bag the rest of his life.

To be honest, I hated the idea of Dad having a colostomy. It tormented me. I'm not even quite sure why it bothered me so much. After all, the procedure could get rid of the cancer. Dad was more positive than I was. He often said, "At least I can *live* with a colostomy." He was right, but I still didn't like it.

After two months, the doctors ordered another scan. The tumor had continued to shrink, but it was still too low, which meant a colostomy was the only option. During that season, every time I looked at Dad, I thought about him having a colostomy bag. I was disappointed, frustrated, and, in a sense, heartbroken all at the same time. It felt like a huge weight on me. I was sad for him and angry at cancer. But I fought to maintain optimism and positivity.

How did I handle it? The same way Shadrach, Meshach, and Abednego did. The only way I knew how. Step. Step. Step. One foot in front of the other. Prayerful always. Yes, the fire seemed hot, but the One who was with me and in me was greater (1 John 4:4). He was equipping me to walk through it.

August 2015

August 13 was the big day. The doctors said the surgery would take up to six hours. I was in Troy that week for classes, so I was unable to be at the hospital. Mom called me throughout the surgery with updates. When all was said and done, the surgery was a success. The surgeons were optimistic that they had gotten it all, but a final scan would be the only way to truly tell. We hoped the doctor was right. In the meantime, step.

The surgery was incredibly intrusive, requiring an extended amount of time for recovery. Dad recovered well. They said he'd remain in the hospital eight to 10 days, but on the fifth day, they released him. His instructions were to rest for six weeks, and then, once his body had time to recover from the surgery, he would begin chemo once again to prevent the cancer from returning. The doctor also scheduled another PET scan to see if Dad was cancer-free.

I've never prayed so hard. A gruesome battle within my heart was taking place every second. I've never wanted anything so badly. All I could think about was the moment, now only weeks away, when we would hear the report. All my focus was on those words that would come out of the doctor's mouth and the picture we'd see of the scan. I couldn't stand the wait. Please, be gone. Please, be gone. Cancer-free would be nothing shy of miraculous, but could it be? From stage IV to cancer-free?

All we could do was wait.

Time went by about as quickly as grass grows in the winter, and that's being generous. On September 23, Dad went back to work and began preaching again that same week. He was building his strength back and doing very well. The PET Scan was scheduled for October 26. In the meantime, I was in Troy fighting through my third semester of college. The day finally came, and the news was not what we were hoping. One lymph node came back positive. Dad still had cancer.

I was crushed. Devastated. Hurt. Confused. Angry. We were so close to all of it being gone. But the cancer was still there, and I faced a level of disappointment I didn't even know was possible.

Perhaps that's what happens when you anchor your hope in an outcome. Perhaps hurt and devastation are a byproduct of locking your hope on something that can change in a second. Since that moment, God has taught me something incredibly crucial. We can't afford to anchor our hope in an outcome or a situation. Outcomes are unpredictable, and situations change. If our hope is set on those things, the moment the outcome isn't what we desire or the situation shifts, we shift with it. In this place, there's no stability and no consistency. The Lord is calling us to a place where we learn to remain in Him (John 15:5) to make His presence our dwelling place—always. All times of the day. In this place, the outcome won't shake us because our ultimate hope is in Him.

Many would say, "But you were hoping for cancer-free, right? That's not a bad thing to hope for!" Well, yeah, that's right. It's not a bad thing to hope for. But when we place our ultimate hope in anything outside of the person of Jesus Christ, we will live influenced by circumstances when we're called to overcome them (John 16:33). The reality is that Jesus was not influenced by circumstances, and He wasn't moved by them. He even slept peacefully in the midst of a life-threatening storm (Matt. 8:24). He learned to keep His heart anchored in His Father. In that place, circumstances would shift, but His peace would remain.

I had become so focused on cancer-free that I had actually taken my eyes off Jesus. Crazy, right? I begged the Lord to take the cancer away, afraid of what would happen if He didn't. It was fear, not faith. I was actually placing my faith in the report instead of in the person of Jesus. I had magnified the words that had come forth from the surgeon's mouth as if those words were a final Supreme Court ruling. I could hear the sound of the gavel striking the desk. In my mind and heart, if the report read anything less than cancer-free, then God had fallen short. How preposterous! The Holy Spirit gently reminded me that a report or anything of the sort could not dethrone God or take His lordship away. Yes, Dad still had cancer. But Jesus is still Lord.

Was our posture different now that we had gotten an outcome we didn't want? Absolutely not! Onward was the only way to go.

November 2015

November 4 marked the beginning of Dad's next chemo cycle. Due to excessive fatigue and neuropathy in Dad's feet, the oncologist opted to go with a different medication with different side effects. It didn't take long for Dad's hair to begin to fall out. Even sooner than that, the nausea began to kick in.

It was a cold night around the end of November, and we were walking out of a basketball game toward the car. I was four or five steps in front of Dad when I heard him throwing up. I turned around to look. Two times, three times he bent over and threw up on the concrete, but he kept walking. Since I had been in Troy, this was the first time I had seen this. It broke my heart; I couldn't stand to watch it, but there was nothing I could do. So, I continued to look for ways to make a positive impact. I continued to be the encourager and tried to always find a positive thing to grab hold of and cling to. Dad would have great days, and then he'd have harder days. I didn't like to classify days as bad days because I felt that was negative. But on those days when I felt as if things couldn't get any worse, positivity was hard to come by. All we could do was wait and pray, hoping the chemo would obliterate the cancer.

February 2016

The waiting game isn't fun. Or at least it wasn't for me. When February rolled around, things seemed to get even scarier. Dad began to have some pain in his leg. He said it felt like a pulled muscle, but it wouldn't get any better. We soon discovered that he had developed a large blood clot in his right leg, and the pain hindered his ability to walk, which presented its own set of problems. If he couldn't walk, his body would lose strength, and he wouldn't be strong enough to take the chemo. Mom had to give him two blood thinner shots daily. That didn't dissolve the clot, but it kept it from getting worse.

March 2016

I thought things couldn't get any worse, but they found a way. March rolled around, and Dad developed a large abscess near the opening of his incision. When he sat, he favored one side to keep his weight off the large abscess. The doctors agreed that the wound needed to be drained to ease the pain. After surgery and a night in the hospital, Dad was released to go home. But things were different. All of the momentum seemed to be heading the wrong way.

April 2016

Just a couple weeks later, Dad began having pain in his abdomen after he ate. My mom called his surgeon, who then sent Dad to Princeton

Hospital in Birmingham, Alabama. By that time, I was back in Troy, so as they rushed to Birmingham, I had no idea anything was happening.

I was sitting in a Dairy Queen when I got the call. It was a Thursday night, and I was having dinner with Chase, one of my good friends. I remember it like it was yesterday—chicken finger basket, fries, and ministry talk. During this season, each time my phone rang, my heart began to race as I hurried to see who was calling. In the two or three seconds it would take to pull my phone out of my pocket and look down to see who it was, worst case scenarios would race through my mind. Is Dad okay? What has happened? "Lord, please don't let it be Mom," I would say to myself. It wasn't that I didn't want to talk to Mom, but I was afraid of the news she might have. I took my phone out of my pocket. It was Mom. Internally, I was in a panic, but somehow I forced out a calm, peaceful, pretend-like-nothing's-wrong hello. Then there was that voice again, the voice I had recognized before—the pretend, calm, collected voice she had mastered. Something was wrong. The 10 seconds of small talk subsided, and she got me up to speed on what had happened. They were sitting at Princeton Hospital in Birmingham. We probably talked five or six minutes on the phone. I'll never forget her exact words, "You may wanna come on up tonight."

It was a Thursday. I had several classes on Friday morning. Why was she telling me to pack up and come to the hospital? That couldn't be good. I agreed without hesitation, told her I'd call her when I left, and then hung up the phone. I told my buddy what had happened, and he immediately prayed with me. My appetite was completely gone, so I didn't finish my meal. I headed back to the dorm and packed up my stuff in a hurry. I grabbed a whole suitcase because I didn't know what was to come. I remember even grabbing my suit and dress shoes, not knowing if I might be attending my dad's funeral before I came back to Troy. I hoped for the best but was prepared for the worst.

During the drive home, I had two hours to just think, which, in a situation like this, could have been a very dangerous thing. If I wasn't careful, I could let my mind drift to only the worst-case scenarios. I called a few of my friends in Birmingham—Alex, Charley, and Jerryn—to let them know what was going on, and they graciously opened their apartments and dorms to me for however long I needed to stay.

I arrived at the hospital, and Mom called and told me where to go. I was relieved to finally be in the same place as my family, but I hated that it had to be there. As I walked into Dad's room, I was greeted with "Hey, Son!" I couldn't help but smile a little as I said, "Hey, Dad." That put me at ease. Dad had a way of doing that. Even if the situation was horrific, just talking to him encouraged me. I sat down in the empty chair beside Mom and heard the story of what happened. As Mom talked and as I looked at Dad, the first thing I noticed was the tube in his nose that seemed to be suctioning liquid from inside of him and dumping it into a canister behind his bed. He had been having tremendous pain when eating. The doctors said he had a blockage in his small intestine from a cancerous tumor. A malignant obstruction, they called it. I knew this was a fancy way of saying the cancer had spread. I remember asking my mom what that meant, and her answer concerned me. "The doctors are going to come in here and tell us the details tomorrow." There was something about the way she said it; I knew she knew something I didn't, but I didn't ask her anything else. She told my brother and me that the doctors were going to meet with us in the morning at 9:00. I took a deep breath. I didn't know what to expect.

I hung out a few more minutes but then wanted to let Dad rest. I headed to Alex's dorm at a nearby college to spend the night. As I lay down that night, I was convinced the doctors were going to tell us how much time Dad had left to live. Three months? Six months? Maybe a year at best? Maybe it was negative thinking, but I couldn't help but think that way. Everything was going so well at first, but it seemed as if we were on a steep downhill slope. I didn't know where the slope was going to take us or where it was going to end.

Morning came, and I wanted to get to the hospital early. I left around 8:30 a.m., early enough to grab a biscuit on the way. I walked into the room, greeted by Dad's "Hey, Son!" I smiled again and replied, "Hey, Dad." Mom grinned at me, and I sat down in the same chair I was in the night before. Mom was to my left, Dad was in front of me, and Kyle was on the other side of Dad's bed. There wasn't much to talk about. We made small talk for a few minutes, but we all knew we were just waiting for the doctors to tell us the latest. It's like time stood still as we watched the clock. Once 9:00 a.m. came, I began peering at the door—9:15, 9:30. Still nothing—9:45, 10:00, 10:30. Still nothing. It was a horrible hour and a half. Then it was 10:45. By that time, it was excruciating and frustrating—then 11:00, 11:15. About that time, the door swung open, and the doctors greeted each of us. The time had come. They had on green scrubs and white coats, each carrying clipboards in their hands. After they introduced themselves and we had a few moments of polite talk, the head surgeon pulled up a stool, sat down with his clipboard, and looked around at each of us. You could tell he was primarily addressing my brother and me, so I knew he had already met with my mom and dad the night before.

He looked down and then looked back up, his eyes bouncing between me and Kyle. He cut straight to the chase, and I'll never forget the words he said. "Barring a miracle, cancer will be what takes your dad to heaven." In that moment, so many thoughts surged through my mind. I felt the tears begin to form in my eyes. Then I felt them work their way down my face and drop onto the floor. In that moment, I battled two enormous thoughts. For the very first time, I felt I had a glimpse of the end, but not the way I wanted it to be. On the other hand, I knew without a shadow of a doubt that God could wipe out the cancer completely with a breath. It wasn't a place of doubt, but it also wasn't a place of denial. Dad had terminal cancer, but Jesus was still Lord. The surgeon, who was trying to describe how

VICTORY

much cancer there was, said it would be like taking a small cup of river rocks and tossing them into my dad's abdomen. "Medically, we cannot do anything to get rid of this cancer. But we all know One who can." He looked at me, then Kyle. "Your dad knows Him, too."

He didn't give us a timeline because he didn't really know how long Dad had left should the cancer run its course. He only began to encourage us. "Cancer doesn't have to be the center of every conversation." His encouragement was to live, to enjoy the season, to make the most of it. After a couple more minutes of sharing his heart, he shook our hands, smiled at each of us, and then walked out of the room.

I looked down and continued to cry. To my left, my mom was crying, and she reached over and placed her hand on my back to comfort me. Across the bed, Kyle was crying. He had been at home for the duration of this journey, seeing firsthand the things I had only heard about. Dad was lying there reclined, relaxed, and smiling as if nothing had changed. How? Well, in his mind, nothing had changed. "All this does is take it out of the hands of man and put it in the hands of God," he said. "And there's no better place for me to be." Talk about an undaunted faith, a faith that had walked through the fire only to be refined and reinforced, a faith that stood the test of trial and didn't fail.

Seeing him and his response to such news wrecked me that day. It gave me a glimpse of what it really looks like to love the Lord and trust Him. I looked intently into Dad's eyes, but I never once saw fear. I listened intently to his tone, but I never heard fear. He knew in whom he believed, and it was in Jesus that His eternity was secure. You see, my dad was never afraid because either way it went, he was going to be all right. Dad didn't dread either outcome. If God destroyed the cancer, praise the Lord. If Dad died, well, he's never going to die (John 11:26). It would only be life forevermore in the place where there is no cancer, the place Jesus had already prepared for him (John 14:3).

Looking back, it reminded me of that January night 15 months before when we received news of the diagnosis. My mom, my brother, and I were a mess. But there was Dad—calm, at peace, and sure. Not sure of the journey or sure of what the outcome would be, but sure that Jesus was Lord and always will be. In two of the toughest moments of my life to that point, Dad remained unmoved.

Perhaps this is the call of God for each of us. Perhaps this is the picture in Daniel 3. No matter how much hotter the fire may get, we are called to walk *through* it. When Jesus rose from the dead, He destroyed any power the fire ever had. So we should not live in a way that gives power to something that has none. We should not bow our thoughts and hearts down in fear at the altar of something that has no power at all. With the empowerment of the Holy Spirit, we will walk *through* the thing that came to destroy us. How do we walk through something? We keep stepping. And that's all we know to do.

After a couple weeks in Princeton, Dad was released to go home. I was back in Troy, and summer was just around the corner. I was lying in bed when I heard the ding from my phone at around 8:00 a.m. It was a text from Mom. "What time do you have class today?" Mom had never asked me that before. She knew my schedule. So I knew something was going on, and I responded quickly. It couldn't have been but a few seconds, and my phone rang. It was Mom. My heart rate spiked in that moment since I knew something had happened. She never called that early.

She didn't beat around the bush—they were at the hospital. Mom had awakened in the middle of the night to find Dad totally unresponsive. After a minute or so of trying to get him to respond, nothing changed. Mom called 9-1-1, woke up Kyle, and waited and prayed until the ambulance arrived. When the paramedics arrived, they checked Dad's blood pressure. It was so low they couldn't even get a reading, and his body temperature was way too high. This was urgent. They grabbed the sheets, moved Dad onto the gurney, and off they went.

Once they got to the hospital, they were able to stabilize him. He was incredibly dehydrated, and the doctors suspected he had an infection from his previous surgery. They were able to get his blood pressure up and his temperature down. Mom had waited to call me until she knew Dad was stable. I was angry—angry that Mom and Kyle had watched all of it happen firsthand and I hadn't been there to help. I was angry that it looked like we were so close to the end of this cancer and now it seemed like nothing could go right.

The fire was hot. I could feel the heat, even three hours away. But there was only one thing I knew to do. Keep stepping. Just like Shadrach, Meshach, and Abednego. Keep stepping. Sitting back in misery wasn't an option. Walking was the only way *through*.

- - - - - - - - - - -

Dad ended up spending five days in the intensive care unit (ICU) and then 11 days in a regular hospital room. All the while, he couldn't go back on chemotherapy, so the cancer was free to spread with no resistance.

Dad seemed to be dodging bullets. Nothing could go right. All hell seemed to be breaking loose.

The Only Way There Is *Through*

David said it this way in one of the most popular psalms ever written:

> *Yea, though I walk* through *the valley of the shadow*
> *of death,*
> *I will fear no evil;*
> *For You are with me.*
> *Your rod and Your staff, they comfort me* (emphasis added).
> —Ps. 23:4

Isaiah prophesied it this way:

> *When you pass through the waters, I will be with you;*
> *And through the rivers, they shall not overflow you.*
> *When you walk through the fire, you shall not be burned.*
> *Nor shall the flame scorch you* (emphasis added).

—Isa. 43:2

I will not pitch a tent and set up camp in the valley I was called to walk *through*. I will step. I will put one foot in front of the other. What enables me to do this? David had the same revelation that Isaiah prophesied about, and we must get it today—God is *with* me. It was the same thing that kept Shadrach, Meshach, and Abednego unharmed and unburned in a fire that would kill anyone within its proximity. It was the same thing that kept the Israelites safe as they ran out of Egyptian slavery into the freedom of God. It was the same thing that empowered David to slay the nine-foot giant that everyone else feared. It was the same thing that empowered Gideon and his 300 men to destroy the much larger, much stronger Midianite army. God was with them! Are we getting the point?

I'll keep going.

It was the same thing that kept Daniel safe and sound after being cast into the den of lions. It was the same thing that equipped Joshua to courageously lead the people of God into the land of promise. And today, it's the same thing that equips us to fulfill the call of God on our lives to walk in the love of God, in the grace of Jesus, and in communion with the Holy Spirit (2 Cor. 13:14), taking the same authority He took back and making disciples of all nations (Matt. 28:19–20). He is with us. Hallelujah!

- - - - - - - - - - - -

The cancer was back—with a vengeance. But our posture must not change. Step. Step. Step. I didn't know whether the Lord would do what medicine says cannot be done. But I knew He could. So I stepped, believing, hoping, trusting. We didn't know what the coming weeks and months held. But we stepped anyway, hand-in-hand with the One who purchased us (1 Cor. 6:20). We put our heads down on the pillow each night and woke up each morning, understanding that there is great purpose in our every breath.

Chapter Seven

BELOW THE SMOKE

My Uncle Terry's house just recently caught on fire. If it hadn't been for the mailman who happened to be passing by on his daily route, it would've burned completely to the ground. My uncle lives right across the street from his mom, my Mawmaw. He was visiting with her when a violent, abrupt knock sounded at the front door. He rushed to the door and was greeted by a panicked mailman who pointed across the street to the clouds of smoke rising through the roof. Terry darted through the yard, across the street, and, without hesitation, rushed into his house to grab what he could. He was in there three, maybe four minutes. By that time, Mawmaw had made her way across the street and was screaming through the doorway at him to get out of the house. With flames covering the ceiling, the sound of electrical wires popping, and smoke filling the entire house, Terry was in extreme danger. The house could cave in at any time. Moments later, the mailman stormed into the burning home, grabbed Terry, and forced him out of the house and into safety. Terry stumbled out, gray from the smoke and coughing up a storm. If he had stayed inside much longer, it could've been much worse. About that time, firefighters arrived on the scene and extinguished the fire before the whole house was engulfed.

Here's the reality: With fire comes smoke—100 percent of the time. In my uncle's case, the fire didn't harm him, but the smoke did. If the cough didn't let you know he'd been inside, you could just look at him and tell from the gray residue, the smell of smoke, and the bloodshot eyes. It couldn't have been more obvious!

Interestingly, this wasn't the case with the three Hebrew boys in Daniel 3. King Nebuchadnezzar called Shadrach, Meshach, and Abednego out of the furnace. Once they came forth, the multitude of people gathered around them. The sight was extraordinary.

> *The hair of their head was not singed nor were their garments affected, and the smell of fire was not on them.*
> —Dan. 3:27

Insane! This was an incredible miracle that had just taken place. These three men who were cast into a furnace of fire had come out unsinged and unburned, and they didn't even smell like smoke. It was spectacular that they lived but even more amazing that they didn't get burned or smell like smoke. They didn't come out coughing. They weren't covered in the debris from the blaze. They weren't even sweating. In fact, the chains that bound them before they were cast in had been loosed in the fire (Dan. 3:25). They were free! Those who saw them would have never been able to tell they were in the fire.

This remarkable story is packed with significant meaning. It's been preached so many different ways and used countless times to greatly encourage people walking through adversity. Honestly, it's one of my favorite stories in the entire Bible. But the power of the message isn't complete without understanding this: Smoke rises.

Shadrach, Meshach, and Abednego would only *bow* to the one true God (Dan. 3:18). That was something they lived, not something they merely decided to do. It didn't matter how hot the fire was. Let's look at this.

Physically, bowing down is a position in which you posture yourself low to the ground, often on your knees. When Elijah bowed, the Bible says he "put his face between his knees" (1 Kings 18:42). Spiritually, it is a position of humility; it's a posture of worship and adoration. It was in *this* position that the Lord met the three Hebrew boys in the fiery furnace, destroyed any power the fire had, and gave them the strength to walk through it. It all began with bowing only to the one true God.

Shadrach, Meshach, and Abednego modeled the standard we're called to live. In difficult situations or, to put it another way, when life gets hot and it seems as if our house is on fire, the moment we try to stand up is when we begin to inhale dense smoke that makes it painful to breathe. The small particles in the smoke begin to wreak havoc on our airways as we gasp for air. In the same way, the moment we come off our spiritual knees and abandon humility and honor, our ability to see is greatly hindered. We open our eyes only to be greeted by the burn of the hot smoke rumbling through the air. There's no relief in sight, so panic and fear set in. All we can see is a bunch of nothingness as the smoke totally surrounds us. We must get out of the smoke!

There's only one way to do that. We must get back on our knees. Why? Because smoke rises. If we get on our knees, we position ourselves lower than the smoke in the air. When we get below it, there will be a sense of vision, breath, and hope. All of a sudden, we see where we are. The smoke no longer clouds our vision. The small particles no longer cut our airways with each breath. We can even see the door. It's the posture of worship—the posture the three men modeled. It's the place we are called to live our lives.

In my life, it's the place that declares the goodness of God, even when the fire is hot. It's the place that says, "Hope is alive," even when there seems to be no way out. It's the place where God meets me. All of a sudden, I'm not panicked anymore trying to find a way out of the house. Jesus meets me there. The fire is still hot, and there's still a lot of smoke in the air, but it doesn't matter because He's with me. I can enjoy communion with God because the fire has no power over me. If He puts the fire out, praise the Lord. If He decides to let the fire roar, praise the Lord. Either way, my posture determines whether or not the fire affects me. When I can learn to live on my spiritual knees—live my life in prayer, committed daily to the Word of God, committed to getting to know Jesus more—God takes what was meant to destroy me and makes it work for me (Rom. 8:28).

How does this relate to my story? Well, the fire was raging around me, which left me with a choice. Would I learn to live below the smoke? Would I stay prayerful, diligent, and committed? Or would I become consumed with my circumstance and let emotion rule my life? We all have times when we must ask ourselves those very questions.

- - - - - - - - - - -

Dad had a choice to make, too. Go back on chemotherapy? Ride it out and let the cancer run its course? Medically, the chemo couldn't get rid of the cancer, but it might slow it down. If he opted to take the chemo, the fatigue and sickness would decrease his quality of life. The decision was tough, but Dad wasn't going down without a fight. After 11 days in Princeton, he was discharged. He began chemotherapy the next week.

That summer, I was home from Troy, so I got to help with Dad's care. I was so thankful for that! Mom and Kyle had been working so hard, and this was my opportunity to help.

The few summer months were devoted to rebuilding Dad's physical strength. It had been 18 months since the diagnosis, and we were beginning to see the wear and tear on his body in a drastic way. Three times a day, I'd walk alongside Dad through the house as he counted his steps. Then we'd go to his bed and do some light weight resistance training to try to build up his arm strength.

Finally, I'd stand at the foot of the bed and push against his legs as he pressed them forward. Two sets of eight with each leg was always the goal. Some days were great, and he would be full of energy and excitement. Some days were tougher when all he wanted to do was lie down and rest.

It was a roller coaster! I never knew what I'd face each morning. Some days, Dad would be sitting up in the recliner, already bathed, eating a nice breakfast, and watching TV. I was so thrilled when I saw this. Some days, he wouldn't be out of bed until after lunch, and I'd know he wasn't feeling well. Life continued like this, day after day. I wasn't sure if the chemo was working. I wasn't sure if God was going to heal my dad. I wasn't sure how much time I had left with him. I wasn't sure how much longer his body would hold up.

- - - - - - - - - - -

Dad was dealing with neuropathy in his feet, which was a result of his first chemotherapy treatment. His knees didn't seem to have the strength to get him out of bed on his own, so he used a walker to push himself up onto his feet. His back was causing him tremendous pain because of the extended time he spent lying down. Things were tough. Dad was so weak that he was unable to reach behind him or bring a glass of water up to his mouth to drink. But right when we needed it most, some friends we had not seen in years visited Dad.

I need to tell you about the McClellan family—Dr. Mike, Dr. Leslie, and their two kids, Austin and Grace. Dr. Mike and Dr. Leslie were our chiropractors when Kyle and I were growing up. However, as life got busy, we lost touch with them. They had heard about all that was going on with my dad and wanted to come by to see how they could help. From that day forward, Dr. Mike came to our house four to six days a week to adjust Dad using his massage machine and some sort of something else—I'm not really sure. But whatever it was, it worked! Within three days, Dad was able to reach to the side table and drink from a glass by himself. It wasn't much longer until Dad was able to stand up on his own and slowly walk unassisted through the house. It was amazing!

Grace, the chiropractors' daughter, began making signs to place throughout our house. Some of them simply stated goals Dad had set during the journey.

Preach on Father's Day.

Stand up and preach.

Go back to school and teach.

Walk unassisted.

She placed them throughout the bedroom, on the walls, on the furniture. She put them in the hallways where Dad walked; he couldn't go a step without seeing a sign that helped keep him going. Some of them had scripture on them, and some had encouraging words or phrases Dad had used in his sermons:

I can do all things.

He sent His Word and healed me.

Fight victoriously!

Great and *mighty* things!

They served as a constant reminder to push onward and keep stepping. That's all we knew to do.

- - - - - - - - - - -

October 7 was a Friday, and I had been back in Troy all week. Dad was scheduled to have an outpatient surgery to remove his urinary catheter and replace it with a supra pubic catheter.

Initially, my plan was to come home for the weekend and be with my family while Dad had the surgery. The doctors said it would only take 15 minutes followed by a few hours in recovery. Dad would go home the same day. Because it was such a minor surgery, Mom encouraged me to continue with my plans to go with my friend Caleb to Panama City, Florida. We headed to Florida late Thursday night and spent a few hours that night exploring some places in the city. The next morning, we ate a leisurely breakfast, hung out with Caleb's family, and just enjoyed relaxing for a while. Dad's surgery was scheduled for that afternoon. Around 2:00 p.m., we decided we wanted to go fishing in the bay, just down the street from where Caleb lived. I'll never forget it. We were walking down the street toward the water, and I got the weirdest feeling while thinking about Dad's surgery. The word *complication* just kind of dropped into my mind. Looking back, it doesn't make sense why that didn't scare me. But to this day, I believe the Lord spoke it to me. I began to pray for Dad's surgery.

Moments later, my phone rang. It was Mom. Dad was having complications. I stopped in my tracks mid-stride. My heart started pounding, and I felt like I was about to puke. I found myself falling into a squat. Caleb was walking just a few steps ahead of me with one of his fishing buddies. They looked back and asked if I was okay. I forced out a calm one-liner that let them know I'd be there in a minute. Squatting down, I listened as Mom spoke. *Complications. Aspiration.* Those were the two words I remember hearing. She didn't know much, but she said she'd call me back as soon as she knew more. I stood back up and continued to walk toward the water. I had a fishing rod, but I put it aside and sat on the ground near the shoreline, waiting for Mom to call me back and tell me more specifics. In a moment, reality began to set in as I realized how far away I was from home. More than six hours. To make matters worse, I didn't have my car because I had ridden with my friend. So I'm six hours away. In another state. I felt stranded. Could it be any worse?

Mom called again. I answered in a hurry. She still didn't know too much, but Dad had aspirated during surgery, and they were going to keep him overnight as a precaution. I didn't know exactly what that meant, but I could tell by her tone that she was unsure what the next few hours would hold. I asked her if I needed to come home, but she told me to wait a little bit longer to see what we needed to do. She hung up, and I was left there. Alone. Scared. I felt sick. I didn't know what to do. If I was going to have to go home, I needed a way to get there. My car was in Troy, halfway between Panama City and home. I knew if I could get to Troy, I could get my car and head toward the hospital. I hurriedly texted some of my friends in Troy to let them know what was going on. If my mom called, I wanted to already have a plan in place. My roommate, Kevin, was the first to text me back. It turns out he had gone to Dothan for the weekend, which was right above the Florida state line. He agreed to meet me wherever I needed him to be. That was my first connection. Now I had some time to figure out the second part.

The phone rang again—it was Mom. This time, I could hear the fear in her voice. She didn't even try to hide it. I could hear her sobbing between words, trying to muster up the strength to give me the latest update. She had just seen Dad for the first time since surgery, and he was intubated. He was fighting the tube, trying to pull it out, and the nurses had to tie his hands to the hospital bed. Mom was told that he was showing signs of sepsis and pneumonia. His blood pressure was way too low.

He was fighting for his life.

Mom told me I should come home, and I told her I'd find a way. I began to wonder if a flight would be the quickest way back. But if I flew, I wouldn't have a car or any clothes because they were all in Troy. I looked for some last-minute flights for that night, but the nearest airport was more than an hour away, and there weren't any available flights until the next day. By that time, a lot of our family members had made their way to the hospital to be with Mom and Dad. My cousin, who had some connections with private planes, called one of his buddies in Florida to see what he could arrange. It seemed like an eternity waiting to know what I needed to do. In the meantime, Caleb's dad graciously agreed to drive me wherever I needed to go. I began to pack my stuff, knowing that was the best plan for me.

I brought my bag downstairs, and Caleb's family all gave me a big hug. Then we all joined hands and prayed. To be honest, as we were praying, I was scared. Even though they had prepared hamburger steak and a baked potato for me, it was no longer appealing. My appetite was completely gone.

Off we went. Surprisingly, the drive went by rather quickly. We arrived at the state line, and I hopped in with Kevin, who would take me an hour to meet my friend Addison in Ozark. Addison had kindly agreed to drive me the final leg to Troy. Sixty minutes to Ozark. Thirty minutes to Troy. Three hours to the hospital.

It was around 8:00 p.m. when I got a call from my cousin Tony to give me an update. The moment Dad's blood pressure medicine had finished its cycle, his blood pressure had dropped in a hurry—a threatening 40/31—and was still falling. Adding another drip pulled it back up for the time being. Even so, they knew it was only a matter of time until that bag also ran out. He was maxed out. When this bag ran out, there was nothing more they could do.

I was 30 minutes from Ozark when the phone rang again. It was Tony. I'll never forget his words. "It's not looking good, man." Dad was holding on, fighting, but I wasn't sure how much he had left in the tank.

Dr. Mike and Dr. Leslie had come to the hospital when they heard what was going on. I called Dr. Mike's cell phone because I knew he'd be in the room with Dad. When he answered, he said Dad could hear me. Dad was fighting. His blood pressure drip had ended, and immediately, his blood pressure began to fall. It was like someone had hurled a baseball off the top of a stadium—gravity takes over, and there's nothing we can do to stop it. Stopping Dad's numbers from zeroing out would take supernatural intervention.

Dad didn't have long—maybe just minutes to live.

I remember yelling through the phone at Dad. "Fight, Dad! Fight! You can do this!" The buildup of my emotions began to erupt, and tears began to fall. It was the most helpless feeling I've ever had.

"Come on, Dad! Hang in there!" I was screaming into the phone as Kevin was praying alongside me. Dr. Mike said, "He can hear you, Colin, he's hearing you!" I screamed more. I didn't want to lose him. This was not the way this was going to happen. This was not going to be the end. Seconds later, just when I thought things couldn't get any worse, they did. The phone call dropped. I looked at my phone. No service.

No way. This had to be a joke. I had 25 minutes left until I met Addison in Ozark. For an excruciating 25 minutes, I sat there as we drove. Unsure. Kevin was driving as fast as he could, but it was torture. As I sat there, I began to pray in the Spirit. I felt the power of God surging through me with each breath.

After what seemed an eternity, I finally got a bar of service and called back. As it rang, questions were powering through my mind. Did Dad's blood pressure stabilize? Is he still struggling? Is he still alive? That's when they told me the news.

I didn't get the whole story until I arrived at the hospital four hours later.

- - - - - - - - - - - -

Dad's blood pressure had begun to bottom out a second time, and they called the rest of the family back into the room. The doctors thought it was the end. There were 30 family members in one unit watching all this unfold. People began to pray. Dad's numbers were bouncing back and forth. Everyone could see the warfare on the screen. Dad was fighting, people were praying, and the enemy was trying to take out my dad. His blood pressure reached a deathly level and was still falling. Dr. Leslie began to pinch and slap his face to keep him awake, while some in the room were praying in the Spirit. To others in the unit, I'm sure it was a commotion like no other. Many were proclaiming the name of Jesus, knowing He was the only One who could stop what was imminent.

Warfare! It was real. Dad's numbers began to rise. People kept pressing. Kept pressing. Medicine couldn't do it, but his numbers kept climbing. Systolic hit 70. Dr. Leslie excitedly yelled, "Robby, you're at 70! Let's get to 80!" 80. "Let's get to 90." Seconds went by. 90. "Keep going, Robby! 100! You're almost there! Let's get to 110!" 110. "Keep climbing!" 120. "We're not stopping here until we see 130!"

130/88. Stable.

It was truly miraculous. Thirty of my family members had just witnessed firsthand what was nothing shy of a miracle. God had done it again.

- - - - - - - - - - - -

It was a little after midnight when I arrived at the hospital. The elevator doors opened, and there was most of my family and many friends. I smiled as I walked into the waiting room and went over to hug them. Dr. Mike and Dr. Leslie were still there, and I embraced them like I never had before. After talking to everyone for a minute, I went to see Dad. Mom and Kyle were still with him. He was exhausted, and rightfully so. He was on a ventilator so he couldn't talk. But I was thrilled to just see him—and I was thrilled that he was going to be okay.

Looking back now on that night, I can say that it was the hardest night of my entire life. I've never been so scared. Dad was looking death in the face and may have even had one foot in heaven. And I was so far away.

I felt like I was in a burning house with no way out. The fire was hot, the smoke was dense, and the whole thing could come down at any minute. At that moment, I felt like the agonizing pain of helplessness would be too much to bear. But we stayed below the smoke—the Lord met us there and carried us through.

Chapter Eight

HOPE IS BORN

It was a scary night. There were at least 10 of us still in the waiting room. Some slid the waiting room chairs together to make a bed so they could sleep for a while. Every 20 to 30 minutes, I walked nervously back to the surgical intensive care unit (SICU) and took a look at Dad's vitals on the screen, hoping he was hanging on. By that time, I was very familiar with what the numbers meant. Each time, I saw that his blood pressure, pulse, and oxygen levels remained stable. Around 6:00 a.m., Dad was continuing to improve, so I decided to head home and get some rest. We knew we had a long journey ahead of us, but Dad's road to recovery had begun.

As the weeks progressed, we never lost our positivity. We learned to celebrate the little things. Dad started with 10 to 12 drips through IVs. When they took one away, we celebrated. When Dad ate a good meal, we celebrated. When Dad was transferred from SICU to a regular room, we celebrated. When his white blood cell count returned closer to normal, we celebrated. When his white count was too high, well, we'd celebrate that his red blood cell count was normal. A friend of ours, Coach Pruitt, brought doughnuts, and we had a little party. Such a fun time.

I remember one time when Dad had an incredibly low platelet count. For four days, he received platelets through an IV drip. Each day we saw an increase, we celebrated. We celebrated to keep a positive mindset and to think about positive things (Phil. 4:8), but we also celebrated to keep Dad thinking positively. But we were really celebrating because the Lord was the One bringing the increase (1 Cor. 3:6). We were praying, and when He performed the miracle and brought Dad further, it was crucial that we celebrated and maintained thankful hearts!

It was Dad's 15th day in the hospital, and we knew the medical team was thinking about letting him go home within the next few days. His platelet count had returned to nearly normal. His vitals remained strong. His other numbers were consistent. To our surprise, however, the doctor came into the room with a huge announcement. He was letting Dad go home that day! I was thrilled, my mom and brother were thrilled, but nobody was more thrilled than my dad. For days, when the doctors asked if he wanted anything, his consistent response was "I want to go home." In fact, when my pastor, Doug Baker, came to visit, he asked Dad the same question: "What do you want?" Dad answered, "I want God to get me out of the hospital bed so I can go home." And that's exactly what God did! The doctors didn't think he would ever leave the hospital, but we saw firsthand that God was much bigger than a medical prognosis.

Finally, we walked out of the room behind the nurse who was pushing Dad in a wheelchair. My mom, Kyle, and I had Dad's belongings in our hands. As we walked down the hallway, I pulled out my phone and took a selfie of Dad and me. I knew we were in the midst of the miraculous, and I never wanted to forget that moment. Dad thanked his nurses on the way out. By now, he knew most of them well. They wheeled him out of the hospital, and for the first time in 15 days, Dad was outside. With the assistance of a couple security guys, we helped Dad into the car. Next destination: rehab. It was time to build his strength to walk again.

What did we do? We celebrated. We praised God because, yet again, He had done what doctors said couldn't be done!

- - - - - - - - - - - -

Dad stayed in rehab nearly two weeks, and then the day finally came. It was time for him to come home! We had been receiving overwhelming support from many people. While Dad was in rehab, his students had each written an encouraging note on a massive piece of poster board and then signed their names. We took it to him, and all he could do was smile. I stepped in front of the bed with the poster propped behind him and snapped a picture as he held two thumbs up. These moments carried him when he didn't know if he could go any further.

- - - - - - - - - - - -

At home, we faced another huge battle—the biggest one yet. The trauma from this recent surgery meant that Dad needed to build up strength before the chemo treatments could resume. In the meantime, the aggressive cancer cells had been spreading with no restraint. Quickly. That sounds scary as I'm typing it. But you know, it didn't really feel that way. As overwhelming and frightening as it was, something was different. I couldn't quite pinpoint it.

We took each day one step at a time. When I was in Troy, Kyle was right there with Dad, doing anything he could to help. He would assist Dad as he walked through the house. When I was home on weekends, I'd give Kyle a break and become Dad's physical training assistant. We would set goals. Some days, it would be one lap around the house. Other days, it would be eight laps. Each step was a victory. A couple of weeks went by, and Dad got to the point that he didn't have the energy to do it at all. He was tired. His body was weak. He didn't have much fight left in him.

I was back in Troy for classes. It was early November when I got a series of texts from my brother. He was sending them one-by-one, telling me what had happened. I was sitting there reading each one as it came across the screen.

Soo...

We got dad out of bed to take him to the doctor.

They were going to evaluate him to see if he was strong enough to get back on chemo.

He got ready, got down the stairs as he held the rails and propped on me.

We got halfway to the car when his legs gave way.

We couldn't get him down gently, but we were struggling to hold him up.

I called Tim who was working at the house, and he ran over and helped.

We got him down gently and got a wheelchair ready for him.

We got him back inside, and now he's lying down.

As I read the texts, I was frustrated, sad, and angry all at the same time. Once again, I was 200 miles away when they needed me most. I could have helped, but I wasn't there. To make matters worse, that meant his body wasn't capable of handling chemotherapy. His body was losing its strength with each passing day.

In my heart, I knew the end was near. On Wednesday, November 16, I was in my dorm room packing and getting ready to come home for Thanksgiving. We had an entire week off, and I was looking forward to spending extra time with my family. As I was cleaning my room, my phone rang. It was Mom.

She began to share with me that Candace, Dad's nurse practitioner and a close friend of our family, had just come by to evaluate him. She asked him, "What do you want?" His response was, "I want to go back to school to teach the kids, and I want to preach." Candace quickly told him that in order for that to happen, he had to eat and exercise to regain his strength. She further recommended that we consider transferring him from home health to hospice care.

As Mom talked, I knew what that meant. They were going to make his last days as comfortable as possible. I experienced a weird emotion when she told me. I was glad. Mom and Kyle had been working tirelessly to take care of him on their own, but with hospice care, he would have more support, lifting the burden from my mom and brother. I think Mom was expecting me to be really upset, but I wasn't. Like I said, something was different now.

I hung up the phone and knew what I wanted to do. I pulled out my laptop. I wanted to hear Dad preach. I went straight to the church's online page and began to play back my favorite videos of him. I was blown away at how his body had changed in 23 months. He had been a pretty large man—six feet three, 300 pounds. But now, he probably didn't weigh much more than 180 pounds. I listened to the message he preached the Sunday after he was diagnosed. He shared the tough news with his church, but then he preached one of the most powerful messages I've ever heard, a message that set the course for the journey that was ahead.

As I sat there and watched the man I looked up to more than anyone else, I was astounded at his words. He didn't know how the journey would look. He didn't know if he'd be healed of cancer on this side of heaven or if cancer would take his life. But he knew one thing—he knew that Jesus was Lord. He knew that no matter the journey and no matter the outcome, cancer wouldn't win because Jesus already had. During his message, he said, "I don't want my boys laying their heads on their pillows at night worrying about Dad. Dad's okay!"

I began to weep. Almost two years had passed since he said that, but his words still rang just as true. I also knew they would ring just as true in another 23 months. It's a truth that eclipses time. Dad really is okay, no matter what. With each word I heard him speak, I felt a continuing shift taking place within me. God was opening my eyes to a greater reality. He was teaching me a renewed way of thinking (Rom. 12:2). He was showing me the magnitude of the cross and what Jesus truly accomplished for us.

As I cried more and more, I began to truly see what my dad had seen the whole time. Of course I knew Dad was saved and going to heaven; there was never a time in the journey when I doubted that. But for the first time, I truly realized it in my heart to the point where I could celebrate it. I cried tears of joy, rejoicing once again that Jesus made it possible for us to know Him. I began to praise the Lord that He had saved my dad and that He had saved me and my family. I knew without a doubt that even though Dad had only days left on this earth, he would take his last breath, and the next breath would be one of total freedom and total victory. For two hours, I watched sermon after sermon. The depth of his wisdom blew me away. The transcendent peace was nothing shy of remarkable.

- - - - - - - - - - - -

By this time, most people had received news of what was happening with Dad. My high school was having a school-wide Thanksgiving chapel service, and I was scheduled to be the speaker. I already had the message prepared, and I couldn't have been more excited. Then I got a call from my high school administrator, Mrs. Greer, who said, "I know you're scheduled for tomorrow, but we can find somebody else if you would rather." I smiled and said, "There's no better time than now." I truly believed that.

People were watching this journey both near and far. In the midst of the hardest time of my life, I was going to have the opportunity to stand up in front of several hundred people and declare a new reality to which God had opened my eyes. A greater reality. Heaven's reality. I was going to have the chance to stand in front of those who knew the depth of the situation and testify to the goodness of God. I knew that in the moments of our greatest sufferings, God reveals His greatest glory (Rom. 8:18). There truly was no better time than now.

It wasn't long after I got off the phone with Mrs. Greer that Mom called again. She was keeping me in the loop on how Dad was doing. He was declining quickly. Each time I had been asked to preach during this journey, I spoke on the miracles God was doing. Mom knew that. Without specific words, I knew she was letting me know that this was the end. She said, "I don't know if this changes your message or anything, but I just wanted to let you know where we are." For the first time, it didn't change a thing. The message God had birthed in my heart wasn't based on the hope of the miracle I had prayed for, but it had everything to do with a greater miracle that had already taken place on a hill called Calvary. For too long, I had put my ultimate hope in Dad's healing here on earth. But now, God had opened my eyes to the greater miracle—Jesus Christ.

- - - - - - - - - - - -

My friend Gray and I left Troy Thursday night a little before midnight. He was going to stay the night and go to the service with me. After a three-hour drive, we got to Gadsden around 3:30 a.m., and I was scheduled to preach at 8:15 a.m. We slept three and a half hours, and then it was time. I was oddly excited. I knew God was about to do in others what He had done in me.

Everyone at the school—Westbrook Christian School—knew the journey we had been walking. Kyle and I had both graduated from that school. My dad had taught math and coached basketball there, and my mom was still teaching there. As I stood up and walked toward the podium, the Lord helped me understand the weight of the moment. It was one I'll never forget.

- - - - - - - - - - -

I preached from Lamentations 3. The passage speaks of Jeremiah's life and how everything that could have gone wrong in his life had gone wrong. Jeremiah spent the entire first two chapters of the book lamenting and mourning over what had taken place. I found that quite interesting, because many people today do the same thing on a much larger scale. We spend much of our time complaining and grumbling about what circumstances have done to us.

As Jeremiah looked back over his life and dwelled on the many tragedies he had faced, his soul began to sink within him (Lam. 3:20). The more he dwelled on the opposition and the negative things around him, the more downcast he became. Then Jeremiah shared a revelation that was the foundation for my message that morning.

> *This I recall to my mind,*
> *Therefore I have hope.*
> *Through the LORD's mercies we are not consumed,*
> *Because His compassions fail not.*
> *They are new every morning.*
> *Great is Your faithfulness!*
>
> —Lam. 3:21–23

Instead of continuing to linger on the hurt and pain of the past, Jeremiah chose to reposition his focus on a greater reality. Yes, he had walked through horrible, horrible years. Yes, I'm sure he had many days when he didn't feel like going on. But in this pivotal moment, he made the choice to look forward and fix his focus on the mercy, compassion, and faithfulness of our great God. He chose to take his eyes off the rubble around him and look up. In that place, he found the hope he so desperately sought. What God did in Jeremiah, God did in me. Likewise, what God did in Jeremiah and in me, God will do in you!

The Lord taught me that when I dwell on the negative, my mind and emotions fall. He taught me that when I try to overcome the hurt through grit and determination, I've stopped short of the call of God. In the midst of the miserable pain, I must take my eyes off of what's in front of me and place them on the greater reality—the goodness and faithfulness of God.

- - - - - - - - - - - -

It was fitting that it was Thanksgiving chapel. I knew Dad had only days to live. But all I could do was stand there with gratitude and declare the faithfulness of God.

All I felt in my heart was gratitude. All I could do was rejoice. Why? Not because I was in denial of reality; trust me, I was very aware of what was about to take place. I could rejoice because God had taught me a new way of thinking. I had become aware of a greater reality—the same reality my dad had been fully aware of the entire time.

Great is Your faithfulness.

It's out of this cry that eternal hope is born. Eternity is a really long time. Those of us who are saved are never going to die. It's in *that* blessed hope that I'll rejoice all the days of my life!

Chapter Nine

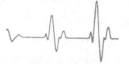

VICTORY

ays had become hours. Dad's health had begun to go downhill at a quicker pace. On Wednesday, he was carrying on a normal conversation, but by Thursday night, he was restless and couldn't get comfortable. By Friday afternoon, he was confused, in and out of a nonresponsive state.

I remember sitting in the living room hearing Dad in pain. He called my mom into the room and asked her to cover him up because he was cold and then said he was hot and asked why she had put a cover on him. Then, trying to find a more comfortable position, he asked mom to slide him over. As she slid him, he grimaced with pain. That was it for me. I couldn't stand it anymore. Nobody wants to see that happen to anyone, but especially when it's your own dad.

I was really amazed watching my mom handle this the only way she knew how, with insurmountable love and great grace. She knew the end was very near. She was gentle, patient, kind, looking to find anything that would make the last few hours the best they could be.

I remember clearly the time when Mom, Kyle, and I were in Dad's bedroom together. It was Saturday morning. Dad was now completely unresponsive. Mom noticed that his sheets were wadded up underneath him. She tried to straighten them, but even the slightest movement caused him pain. She asked Kyle and me to help roll him over so she could straighten the sheets and make it more comfortable for him. Honestly, that didn't make sense to me. Why would we move Dad and risk putting him in more pain just so we could fix the sheets that he didn't even know were wadded? That was the only way she knew to do it—she wanted to be sure he was comfortable. So that's what we did. It was inspiring to watch.

- - - - - - - - - - - -

I had no idea how hard it was on my mom to walk through this journey. She was exhausted. I knew my brother hated seeing Dad in this state. Even more, I knew how tired my dad was. I could see his longing for freedom and for all of this to be behind him. With each painful grimace and moan, I could hear the desperate plea for his new body, his glorious body (1 Cor. 15:54). With each moment of confusion and each struggling breath, I could sense his deep desire for his new home.

Frustrated, I walked into another room, alone. I put both my hands on our pool table, dropped my head, and looked to the floor. In that moment, I knew what I needed to do. I walked into Dad's room, shut the door behind me, and pulled up a chair beside his bed. It was just the two of us. For 30 minutes, I told Dad everything I needed to say. I don't believe he could hear my words, but that didn't matter. I thanked him. I looked back over the course of my life and thanked him for the moments he helped me, the moments he disciplined me, the moments he fathered me. I thanked him for the moments he had been right there, the tough seasons he'd walked with me. I thanked him for the things he had taught me, both small and big. Yes, it was hard. I cried. When I didn't think I could cry anymore, I somehow found a way. But with each word, I gained more peace in my heart. When I finished, I stood up and put both my hands on his leg and closed my eyes. Through my tears, I prayed, "Lord, take him home." I looked over Dad's body and then up at his face. I smiled. I had peace in my heart. I knew that in the Lord's hands was the best place he could be.

- - - - - - - - - - - -

Hospice came Saturday mid-morning and checked his vitals. His blood pressure was continuing to fall at a steady rate. Two days before, the numbers were normal, but they had since fallen to 80/60. His heart rate was climbing a little each day, which is what the nurses had told us would happen.

On Saturday evening, Mom and I were sitting next to Dad, just spending time with him. His blood pressure was now at 60/40. I asked Mom, "Will we take him back to the hospital or just let him go here?" She looked at me with sincere eyes, "Right here." I agreed with her.

At that point, we had to make some hard decisions regarding funeral preparations. We made a list of who would be pallbearers and who would play a part in the service. Then we had to decide on the person we would ask to speak at the ceremony. As she pondered it, we both agreed that Dad's long-time friend Taylor Gallman would be the one to officiate. Taylor, a pastor himself, and his family—Jenny, Andrea, and Nathan—had walked this entire journey with us. He had been there the week we found out the news of Dad's cancer. He had been at the hospital by Dad's bedside the night Dad had nearly died. He had prayed with us through the hard times and celebrated with us in the great times. Their relationship hadn't just begun during this journey. For years, he and Dad had sat beside each other during Friday night football games and talked about the Lord. I can recall numerous times when Kyle and I would be struggling with something, and Dad would call Taylor to come and pray for us. There was no one more fitting to officiate.

Mom then looked at me again as if to ask, "Who else?" I looked at her and grinned. "I am." God had prepared me for this moment.

Just that week, God had given me the opportunity in the midst of the toughest journey of my life to declare the goodness and faithfulness of God to students and teachers of all ages. Now He was giving me another opportunity on the back side of the journey to declare the very same thing. I was excited. I sat there on the bed next to Dad. I had never preached a funeral before. Quite frankly, I didn't even know where to start. But as I prayed, the Holy Spirit began to reveal the way, and as He spoke, I wrote.

That night, I slept in the living room, which was next to Dad's room. I fully expected him to pass during the night. I woke up several times, listening intently to see if he was still breathing. His breathing was slow, but it was still rather loud. I got off the couch early that morning. Dad was still breathing, but with each hour, his breaths became shallower. His blood pressure continued its steady decline, now 50/30. His heart rate was continuing to rise, but it was becoming fainter.

It was truly amazing. In these last days, Dad seemed to be so at peace. Saturday and Sunday, he never once grimaced in pain. He never stirred or seemed uncomfortable. The nurses had brought oxygen to the house for him, but he never needed it. The Lord's hand was upon him.

November 20, 2016

It was Sunday night. There were nine of us in Mom and Dad's bedroom. Hours had become minutes, and in my heart, I knew the moment I had dreaded for nearly two years was here. We watched intently as Dad's breathing grew quieter. We could no longer hear each breath, but we watched his chest barely rise as he worked his way toward his last. I reached down to his feet to find that they were washed out in color and cold to the touch. Here we were, together as a family.

Minutes became seconds.

In a moment, the past 23 months surged through my mind. I thought back to the night of January 3, 2015, when the Lord spoke to me and told me I wouldn't be moved. I thought back to the call I got when Dad's liver had miraculously cleared. I thought back to the time I rushed back to Gadsden from Florida, unsure whether Dad would be alive when I got there. I thought back to both the good moments and the scary moments. But in this moment, here I stood, looking at my dad's nearly lifeless body, and as I looked, there was a smile on my face. It won't make sense to most. In fact, it may seem even twisted to some. But I was looking from a different perspective. In a secret place, God had rewired my way of thinking and opened my eyes to a greater reality. I wasn't moved. I stood between my mom and my brother with my arms around them. As I watched Dad take his final breath, I knew that his breathing never stopped. As he exhaled for the final time here, an inhale took place in another dimension (2 Cor. 5:8). That breath had no cancer in it, and it had no sorrow. That breath was saturated in freedom from pain and agony. That breath was without struggle. That breath marked the beginning of an eternity in the place that was prepared for him (John 14:3).

As I stood in his pulpit to preach his funeral, there was a resounding theme in the message the Lord gave me.

Victory!

Some would say cancer won. I'd beg to differ. It may have *thought* it won. The Roman soldiers thought they had won, too, but the resurrection of our Messiah blasted that theory into oblivion. The moment my dad stood before His maker, there was the blood of a spotless lamb still covering the mercy seat (Heb. 9:12). The blood of Jesus stood on my dad's behalf, destroying any power the cancer had, and Dad walked through the gates of glory, totally healed.

Some would say Dad lost his battle. People who watch others die from cancer use this phrase all the time—"They lost their battle to cancer." I'd beg to differ. My dad didn't lose his battle; he won. He won it the moment he gave his life to Jesus. Some would argue, "But he died." No, he didn't. Death was destroyed the moment Jesus breathed again in the tomb. He defeated death, took back the keys, triumphed over it, and then made a mockery of it. Death has forever been swallowed up in victory. Hallelujah!

> *So when this corruptible has put on incorruption, and this mortal has put on immortality, then shall be brought to pass the saying that is written: "Death is swallowed up in victory."*
>
> *"O Death, where is your sting? O Hades, where is your victory?"*
>
> *The sting of death is sin, and the strength of sin is the law. But thanks be to God, who gives us the victory through our Lord Jesus Christ.*
>
> —1 Cor. 15:54–57

Death and its sting have been defeated once and for all. In Jesus and through Jesus, death is not even a reality. We who are in Christ have life forevermore. We are totally victorious.

- - - - - - - - - - - -

As I shared my heart with the hundreds of people at the funeral, I walked back through the journey. We had experienced so many miracles over those 23 months. When I looked at what the Lord had done, all I wanted to do was shout. All I wanted to do was rejoice! You see, Dad was never supposed to be able to have surgery to remove the colon cancer, but he did. He wasn't supposed to live to see the next day when complications arose during his outpatient surgery, but the Lord did what medicine couldn't do, and he did. After that, his life here was supposed to end in the hospital, but 15 days later, God did it once again, and Dad went home to spend the last part of his life with his family whom he loved so much.

Even with all of this, the greatest miracle of all took place on November 20 at 10:54 p.m. when death visited his body. It intended to claim him, but it was immediately swallowed up in victory! God intervened by becoming flesh more than 2,000 years ago and by paying the ultimate price to secure our eternal redemption. What a glorious triumph!

The Lord had impressed my heart with that one word: *victory*. It would be easy to look back over the course of the journey and dwell on the tough days and the bad things that had taken place. It would be easy to dwell on how badly I miss my dad and place all my focus on the years to come when he wouldn't be with me. But I could hear the whisper of the Holy Spirit reminding me that God doesn't see it that way.

From the pulpit, I looked to my right, directly at my family. There were 30 or 40 of them sitting in the first four rows. Under the direction of the Holy Spirit, I charged them as the Lord had charged me. We have a choice—to sit back in depression, hurt, and confusion for years to come, or to press forward in joy, understanding that death isn't the end. For the saved child of God, it's only the beginning of life with the One who loved us first (1 John 4:19). And the best part? It's never going to end.

As I watched Dad walk through this journey, I learned many things. There are three that stand out above the rest.

He Showed Us How to Walk in Peace

Dad's peace was pretty scary sometimes. In life's scariest moments, Dad didn't seem to budge. There was something within him that was greater than what was around him. We see a similar story in Matthew 8 when Jesus was asleep in the boat during a life-threatening storm. The miracle is about Jesus calming the storm. But perhaps the greater miracle was the fact that Jesus was sleeping while the storm was raging. His disciples were in a panic, believing their lives were about to end. How is that possible? The peace within Jesus was much greater than the chaos caused by the storm around Him.

I'm reminded of a scripture in Isaiah 26:3:

> *You will keep him in perfect peace,*
> *Whose mind is stayed on You,*
> *Because he trusts in You.*

Dad walked in such tremendous peace, but only because He lived with his gaze, his thoughts, his eyes, his life fixed on Jesus. We are called to do the same.

His Joy Wasn't Dictated by His Circumstances

Dad was always joyful, even in times when joy didn't seem possible. Here's the reality. Circumstances change, but that doesn't mean we have to change. If we are looking to our circumstances for joy, then we are going to be disappointed time and time again.

There is a place we can look that will never change. There's a vantage point we can fix our eyes on, and it's the person of Jesus and the salvation of our souls. We rejoice not because life is great and nothing is wrong at the time, but because our names are written in the Book of Life (Luke 10:20). Once we learn to focus on that incredible truth, all we will want to do is rejoice. Why? Because Jesus loves us and saved us. And no matter what comes our way in this life, that will never change. So we can always be joyful (1 Thess. 5:16).

He Showed Us How to Fight Victoriously

It was June, months before Dad passed away. Kyle and I were running a Barbarian Challenge with the McClellan family. It was a brutal one—more than six miles, 32 obstacles through a dreaded terrain. Kyle finished a few minutes before I did, and we were both awarded medals for finishing the race.

Father's Day was the next day, and we both knew the perfect gift. We placed the medals in a shadow box beside a picture of Kyle and me after the race. Underneath, we wrote, "We did it for you, Dad." Across the top was this: "Fight Victoriously." When we gave it to him, he began to cry and said, "This is my favorite gift I've ever been given."

Dad understood that being victorious didn't ride on whether or not the report was good. In the end, he understood that his triumph didn't hinge on whether or not cancer left his body. He understood that He had won the moment he had given his life to Jesus Christ. Paul wrote, "Now thanks be to God who always leads us in triumph in Christ" (2 Cor. 2:14).

Triumph is not something God is taking us toward; it's something He's leading us in. Victory is our ever-present, freedom-restoring, life-giving foundation we stand upon and rejoice in. We are victorious!

Chapter Ten

LIVING FROM ETERNITY

As I'm writing this, it's been nearly two years since Dad joined Jesus in glory. Oh, how glorious it must be to celebrate two years of being home! It's crazy to think about eternity. In our minds, we try to comprehend a million years or even 10 million years. Maybe we think even further to 10 billion or 100 trillion years. But even then, we won't be any closer to the end than when we first began because there is no end. The people of God will dwell there forever!

- - - - - - - - - - - -

The past two years have been a wild ride. I graduated from college, took a full-time job, bought a house, and married my beautiful wife, Lauren, all within about three months. The Lord has been taking me—and now us—on an incredible journey!

For years, I knew in my mind that when the right woman came along, Dad would be able to confirm that she was the right one for me. In past relationships, he just had some crazy way of knowing whether or not it was going to work, and he had been right every time. Now that he was gone, how would I know?

I met Lauren eight months after Dad went to be with the Lord. Anyone who knew my dad knew that his favorite color was purple. He wore purple ties, painted his and Mom's bathroom purple, and even wanted to change the color of the church's pews to purple. Slightly extreme, if you ask me, but he was passionate about it.

When I met Lauren, she had been a hairdresser for six years. One afternoon, a week after we had agreed that we were getting married, she sent me a random picture while we were texting. I looked closely and saw a strand of color in her hair. It was purple. The Holy Spirit clinched my heart. I looked at it closer, and I was blown away. I didn't need Dad's blessing; I only needed the Lord's. But the Lord knew I also wanted Dad's. God whispered to me and made it clear—this was Dad's marked blessing upon her.

The night before our wedding, Lauren and I met the groomsmen, bridesmaids, and family at the church where the ceremony would take place. Mom got there a little early, as we did. She walked into the church, and the first thing she noticed was the pews—they were purple. Dad wasn't there to celebrate with us, but the Lord in His great goodness marked that day with both His blessing and my dad's. I'm forever thankful.

- - - - - - - - - - -

When I met Lauren, my life was changed forever in the best way possible. But I carried a great deal of hurt with me because Dad would never get to meet her. I talked to the Lord about it all the time. There was one morning that changed it all. I'll never forget it.

I was walking around praying. Things were so different. Even though I had tremendous peace about where we were and the work that God was accomplishing in my family, I still struggled immensely with the fact that Dad wouldn't be able to meet my wife. It was a source of a lot of frustration and hurt. Through my tears, I told the Lord, as I had told Him many times before, "Lord, I really wanted

Dad to meet my wife." The Holy Spirit stopped me in my tracks. It was like a thump in the deepest part of my chest. Immediately, He whispered two words that shifted it all: "He will."

I broke. Wow! Here I was, thinking that this huge dream was stripped from me, but in reality, it was a dream that will be fulfilled entirely. In a moment, everything shifted inside of me as I realized that I'll have a lot longer *with* Dad than I ever had *without* him. And my wife and children will also have a *lot* longer to spend with him than without him. We'll have a lot more meals in glory than we could ever share together here. I began to rejoice and celebrate. With this fresh understanding came overwhelming joy.

The Lord had brought about a marvelous transformation in my heart, and I truly hoped that my mom and brother were in a great place, too. They seemed to be, but we really didn't talk too much about what was going on, so I deeply and consistently worried about them. We all knew that Dad was saved and that now he was totally healed. It wasn't a matter of Dad's salvation but rather how Mom and Kyle were dealing with the loss. I spent a lot of time praying for them, and I asked God to give them the same peace He had given me. Soon I came to realize that in the same way God was working in my heart, He was also working in theirs.

- - - - - - - - - - - -

A few weeks after Dad died and the funeral was behind us, we completed all the paperwork and began the road to a new routine. It was morning, and Mom decided to take down all the signs we had put on the walls during the journey. There were probably 30 of them. All the emotions rushed back in a hurry as the memories flooded her mind. That's when the Lord stepped in.

Mom sat down and began to go through Dad's text messages and various things people had sent him along the journey. She stumbled on his email account and unread messages. As she was reading through them, she came across one he had received the morning of the 20th, the day he passed away. Mom clicked on the email—a subscription to a daily devotional—and read the title of the devotion for November 20: "Five Reasons Death is Gain." Wow! God is faithful! Right on time.

> *For to me to live is Christ, and to die is gain.*
> —Phil. 1:21 KJV

The Lord's attention to detail and His deep, authentic care about everything in our lives are overwhelming in the most amazing ways. He had already shifted my perspective and taught me a new way of seeing. When I became overwhelmed with hurt about Dad not being able to meet my wife, the Lord visited me and shifted everything with a fresh revelation. But He didn't stop there. He knew I was still dealing with worry about my mom. When I didn't even know it, He was already working behind the scenes, releasing the same peace to her as He had to me. How crazy it was for me to worry! God is really good at being God, and that day, I learned to trust Him even more. God knows what thoughts and internal struggles we deal with. His heart is to speak truth over us, setting us free each and every time.

There's more. The Lord had spoken to Mom clearly through this devotion on the back end of the journey. She just recently shared with me what the Lord had done for her before the journey ever began. I'll let her words tell the story:

> I have a devotion that comes on my phone each morning. When January 1st rolled around, for some reason, my phone did not change to a new year and was stuck on December 31. So I saw the same devotion on December 31st, January 1st, 2nd, and 3rd. It came from Psalm 39:7:
>
> "My hope is in You."

The morning of January 4th, which was the morning after Robby was diagnosed, the same thing happened. But this time, I saw this scripture with new meaning. The Lord knew what I needed at that time. The next morning, the 5th, my phone's date set back to the right place, and I began getting devotions for January. Psalm 39:7 has been something I go back to often.

Later in that same month, an old friend of Robby received news of him being sick. He sent us a silver Christmas ornament that simply said "Hope." We hung it on our bedroom door, and each time I'd see it, I'd be reminded where my hope is found.

- - - - - - - - - - - -

I must tell this story, as well. To this day, it wrecks me.

It was April 2016, the month my dad's cancer was diagnosed as terminal. Kyle was one month away from graduating from high school. He had already been accepted to Troy University, and after long hours of studying, test prep, and a ton of hard work, he was given a full-tuition scholarship.

That morning of the terminal diagnosis, we sat around Dad's hospital bed and cried for 10 to 15 minutes as the news settled. Kyle and I then stepped out of the room because they were going to bathe Dad. We had a conversation that I'll never forget. He looked at me and said, "I can't go to Troy. I want to stay here and help Mom and Dad." His words astounded me. He was going to give up a free education he had worked so hard to get so he could stay and help Mom and Dad. I looked back at him, smiled, and said, "What will you do?" He didn't know what the future held, but he was sure of this first step.

He waited a week or two after Dad was released from the hospital to share with both of them what he wanted to do. Mom and Dad were both hesitant since they wanted him to do what he had worked so hard for. And Troy's scholarship was only for entering freshmen. If he passed it up, he was passing up his only way to go to Troy. He had applied to a local community college, but he had not heard back. The conversation ended with uncertainty, and they agreed to think about it.

That night, Mom walked out to the mailbox to get the mail. Back inside, she sat down to go through the mail and found a letter addressed to Kyle from the local college he had applied to—Gadsden State Community College. The letter informed Kyle that GSCC was awarding him a full scholarship.

As I write this, I'm weeping in awe of the greatness of God. I'm celebrating the reality that God is for us and that He will part the waters for those who are obedient in the stepping.

Hang on, it gets even better.

That week, Kyle called Troy University's admissions office and explained the situation. Without hesitation, the head of admissions agreed to honor his full-tuition scholarship the following year. Kyle attended GSCC while he stayed home for a year to help Mom and Dad. At the time of this writing, Kyle is a junior at Troy University, studying math education with dreams of continuing in the way Dad started—as a math teacher and basketball coach. Doors have already opened, and the favor of God is outrageous. Hallelujah!

The Writing Begins

A few months after Dad's diagnosis in January 2015, I was in a church service in central Alabama. During the service, they showed a video of a man sharing his testimony. It was remarkable! He had been given a terminal cancer diagnosis. After church members had prayed, he had gone back to the doctor to find that his scans were completely clear. I began to weep as I listened to him share. In that moment, the Lord began to stir in my heart a desire to write about the journey we were on. So that's what I did.

I wanted to write a spoken word, a poem that is recited and typically uses rhyme. Multiple times a week, I sat down and wrote, never knowing exactly how it would turn out. I began telling the story, one event after another. The hard times, the great times. The miracles God performed week after week, and the prayers that I felt went unanswered. It took several months to write, but I finally finished. It was December 2015 when I met my friend Charley and asked him to film the final product. He set up a couple cameras and studio lights, and then I began to orate the message. We edited the video and put the final file on a DVD.

I wanted this to be a gift for Mom and Dad. With Christmas only a week away, I put it aside for Christmas morning. After all the gifts had been opened that morning, I grabbed the DVD and put it in the television so we could watch it together. It wasn't long before Mom was trying to harness her tears. Dad followed suit but kept a proud smile on his face the entire time. Kyle and I tried not to cry, but we couldn't help it. As we continued to watch, I looked back and forth at Mom and Dad, their eyes glued to the screen the entire time. As it drew to an end, we heard the final line of the poem:

God has cleared my vision and helped me see that because of the cross, my dad is cancer-free.

At that time, Dad still had cancer in his body. But I believed God was going to do a miracle. When Dad went to be with the Lord, God began to stir in my heart to revisit the spoken word I had written a year before and to revise and refilm it with the updated story. Since that time, a lot of new events occurred, and honestly, the greatest change of all was within me. God gave me a new understanding and a greater perspective. In the natural, I didn't even know where to start, but as I began to write, direction and wisdom flooded me all at once. At first, I thought to myself, "Well, I have to change the way I ended the poem because it didn't happen that way." The Holy

Spirit checked me again, "Yes, it did." Because of the cross, my dad *is* cancer-free. Forevermore.

The Lord continued to open my eyes to that reality, and I continued to write. It was late January 2016, and I only had a few stanzas remaining. As I sat down to finish, the words came together perfectly. Here is what I wrote.

> I stand here today celebrating the great miracle that's taken place, full of peace, full of joy, with a big smile across my face.
>
> I rejoice in the cross, and I shout VICTORY at His throne, because my dad is healed, restored, set free. He's home.
>
> I called the poem "Victory" because my dad is incredibly victorious.

Nothing had changed. When I wrote 12 months before that Dad would be cancer-free, I truly believed it. But even now in his death, it's all the more true. Dad *is* healed. Every day. For all eternity.

- - - - - - - - - - -

After spending a weekend filming the final spoken word with my two friends Andrew and Gray, the time came for its release. It was the first week of February 2017, and I could not have been more excited. My continued prayer was that the Lord would use it however He pleased.

Within minutes of posting it, my phone was blowing up with social media notifications and text messages. People were being encouraged and uplifted. In the comments, many were tagging their loved ones who were walking through similar journeys, pointing them to the steadfast hope we have in Jesus Christ. Hundreds of people shared the video, encouraging others to watch. Some quoted the phrase from the video that spoke to them the most. I was encouraged because phrases that seemed not as good to me actually became what brought some people to their greatest breakthrough. Within a couple days, it had thousands of views. But it didn't stop there. I was getting phone calls from churches and ministries across various denominations that wanted me to come and speak to their church or group: Baptist, Methodist, Pentecostal, men's and women's ministries, college ministries, philanthropy events, youth rallies, children's events. It was really overwhelming. I could not have been more thankful for the opportunity to tell more people about what God had done.

Two weeks after the release of the video, I got a message from a local magazine in our area. They wanted my dad's story to be the front cover of their March copy. I was blown away! And that's exactly what happened. They did a spread telling the whole story, including the script of the poem I had written. Even more people got to hear the testimony. God is good!

- - - - - - - - - - - -

Over the next six months, I was blessed with the opportunity to share at churches, campuses, and schools with people of all ages and from all walks of life. It's amazing how the message and truth of the gospel of Jesus spans all denominations and ages. Jesus came to save, and everyone needs to know Him. Period!

Following are my personal accounts of just a few of the many things God did during this special season. There is tremendous power in testimony. He gets all the glory!

- - - - - - - - - - - -

I had the opportunity to share at a vacation Bible school at a country church in North Alabama. There were about 120 kids present. All I knew to share was the cross of Jesus, so that's what I did! Because of Jesus's cross and resurrection, we have an invitation to life forevermore.

After I finished, I gave the kids the opportunity to give their lives to Jesus. More than 30 of them came forward. I asked the pastor and a few other adults to come and help me pray with those who huddled together in front by the stage. I felt we needed to pray with each child individually as they took their first step into the calling on their lives. It was amazing! Afterward, the pastor and I talked for a few minutes. Through his tears, he said the church had been praying a long time for a move of the Holy Spirit on their young people. I rejoiced because God was using my dad's story to bring real hope and the life-changing truth of Jesus into people's lives.

- - - - - - - - - - -

I got the opportunity to share at Relay for Life, a cancer awareness event where many people come together to celebrate cancer survivors and also remember those who have passed away. There were more than 500 college students and families gathered across the quad, many of whom had been directly impacted by cancer, just as my family had. I was very nervous, but I was also very excited. Before I came to the stage, they showed the spoken word on a large screen. Then I had the opportunity to share the gospel. Once again, I shared the only thing I knew to share—the cross and the hope we have in Jesus. After just a couple minutes, I heard to my right a young woman crying. In my heart, I knew she had walked a similar journey. From the stage, I asked her how long it had been since she had walked it. Through her tears, she let me know that only two weeks before, her mom had passed away from cancer. After we finished that night, I encouraged her with the same truths that God had spoken to me. Tragedy becomes triumph when we walk in Him. God continued to move and encourage.

- - - - - - - - - - -

In July, I was speaking at a high school leadership seminar where 300 high school sophomores from all over the state were gathered in one auditorium. The title of the message the Lord gave me was "Purpose to Purpose." I poured my heart out about how we can't afford to ever live a day outside of the purpose God has placed on our lives. I shared for maybe 20 minutes, prayed a prayer of blessing over the kids, and brought my part to a close. Afterward, one of the young men came to me weeping and questioning the call of God on His life. He was spiritually hungry and desperate. God brought victory to his life that morning in an extraordinary way! There may not have been 100 people who got saved, but this one young man received the victory Jesus purchased—and that's worth celebrating.

- - - - - - - - - - - -

I was asked to speak to a youth group that had recently lost a classmate to cancer. The boy who passed away was a good friend to many, and these kids were at a crossroads. I shared my heart with the 30 kids in the room, and honestly, it didn't seem like they had a care in the world about what I was saying. I really struggled with that. These young people needed this hope I was sharing.

Through this experience, God taught me that I'm not called to preach to save people. If I just share the good news that has changed my life, He'll bring the increase (1 Cor. 3:7). I finished the message, and if I can continue being honest, I was a bit frustrated. As I walked out the door of the church, I had no idea if even one person had received it. I drove back home with a few friends who had come with me, still completely unsure whether anyone had been impacted.

That night, the youth pastor texted me to let me know that many of his youth texted him about how the Lord had greatly encouraged them. I was so thankful. But it goes even further than that. A few months later, I got a text from the same youth pastor. Each year, he hosted a youth retreat in Panama City, Florida, and he wanted to meet with me about speaking at the upcoming retreat. After much prayer, we both believed the Lord was leading us to go forward with it, so we did.

There were about 500 people packed into the retreat room just off the beach, and I was the first speaker. Before I spoke, they played the video of the spoken word, and then I stood to share my heart. I shared the only thing I knew to share—Jesus and His cross. I preached from John 14, one of the most quoted passages in all of scripture, but the Lord had given fresh revelation that really brought it to life within me in a new way. I preached from this reality: Jesus died so we could be together again. That's what He has cared about since the very beginning, a relationship and communion with the ones He loves. The words may not have been profound, but it was the gospel. About 35 kids came forward and declared Jesus the Lord of their lives. To that, I'll say hallelujah!

I was amazed. Not only did God give me new perspective, but He was using this new perspective to minister the same truth to other people. And He was launching me into the calling He had placed on my life.

- - - - - - - - - - - -

It had been six months since Dad had passed away when I was invited to preach at a church not too far from where I live. From the get-go, the Spirit of God was moving mightily. It was one of the most remarkable services I had ever been part of. As worship began, the Lord gave visions to some of the people in the audience. I remember it clearly. Three people had three different visions simultaneously that all linked together like a puzzle. Each of them built on the other as they each shared what God had shown them. When the third person stood to share her vision, she told us that the Lord has commissioned us to manifest His kingdom. My eyes got big, and my heart began to pound. I looked down at the sheet of paper with my outline on it. The title of my message was "Manifest His Kingdom." That was the phrase God had given me in prayer two days before. He was up to something. As I preached, the people began to respond. I could sense tremendous freedom as the unchanging truth of the gospel went forth.

The service was drawing to a close when Pastor Todd stood up and told the people that I'd be available to pray for them. People lined up in the middle aisle all the way to the back wall. For two hours, the Lord ministered in tremendous ways. With each prophetic word, He was revealing His great love for each person. We prayed, we loved on people, we encouraged families. Two of my great friends, Gray and Parker, were right there with me. After two hours had passed, we were still standing there praying with individuals, couples, and kids. People were making their way into the church for the evening service, and we were still praying. It was incredible! But that didn't stop us, and it sure didn't stop God from continuing to love on His people. We moved to the cafeteria and continued to minister to the people who had waited so long for prayer. After we finished, there were 100 to 120 people the Lord had spoken to, both specifically and prophetically. It was truly amazing. I thought we were done and I was preparing to leave when Pastor Todd and his wife, Lorie, began to pray and prophesy over me.

I'll never forget something she said to me. "Satan knows he's made a mistake. If he could raise your dad from the dead, he would." I began to cry. But they weren't sad tears; they were tears of joy because the glory of God was being revealed.

I began to see the magnitude of what the Lord was doing. He truly was taking a tough situation and turning it into tremendous good (Rom. 8:28). The temporary weight of struggle and suffering had given birth to a much heavier, much more rewarding eternal weight of glory (2 Cor. 4:17). People were being touched. Kids were seeing the great depth of the love and goodness of God toward them. My family and I were encouraged daily by the work of God through what some would call a tragic time.

With all of that in mind, I don't see my dad's passing as a tragedy. It truly is triumph. I look back, and yes, of course I wish Dad were here, but I know that he wouldn't trade where he is for anything in the world. When I live my life from an eternal perspective, I see that my dad is eternally secure, and people are getting saved and stepping into their purpose. Through this journey, God is teaching people to see the way He sees. So I rejoice!

- - - - - - - - - - - -

It was my senior year of college, and I was sitting in my dorm room. Classes were done for the day, and I had some free time to just relax. I sat back on my bed and began to spend some time in prayer and worship. Only a few minutes went by, and I heard the Holy Spirit speak to me: "I'm going to release victory everywhere you go." Wow! That jolted me. I looked back over what God had done each time I shared the story with people, and He had released victory. With joy in my heart, I began to dream about the coming months and years. I knew one thing. God was going to release victory everywhere. I believe that's His heart for every Christian. We are a victorious people!

The next week, I was talking to Lauren on the phone before I went to sleep. While she was in prayer, the Lord led her to look up what each of our names meant. I had never thought about doing that before, so I was excited to hear what they meant. As she told me the meaning of "Colin," I grinned in awe. Colin means "people's victory."

- - - - - - - - - - - -

As I look back over the journey, I choose to remember the great things. I remember when Dad, while recovering from major surgery, made it a goal to get strong enough to preach on Father's Day. He did it. I remember the time when his body was so weak he couldn't stand on his own, but he made it a goal to build strength and be able to *stand* in the pulpit and preach. He did it. I remember the times He persevered in adversity and the times that miracles took place before our eyes.

Most of all, I remember Jesus. Because of Him, death is not the end. In fact, for those who are born again, death is only a passageway into eternal life. I'll run this race the only way I know how—with great endurance and with my eyes on Jesus. As I step in relationship with Him, God will release victory everywhere I go, and Jesus will be glorified.

- - - - - - - - - - - -

Perspective is everything. The heartbeat of God is to rewire our way of seeing so we can see the way He sees, from eternity's perspective. It would be foolish to think we could have a mountaintop view looking from the deepest part of the valley. We must get to the mountaintop. That poses the all-important question that must be answered: *How do we get there?* I'm excited to answer.

Chapter Eleven

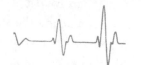

THE WAY UP

It was 4:30 a.m. and cold, down near 10 degrees. The chance to watch the sun make its appearance over Half Dome in Yosemite National Park doesn't come very often. It was time to get up and make our way to Tunnel View where we would be able to watch the beauty unfold.

Earlier that week, I had flown to Los Angeles with seven of my best friends from college, and we had mapped out a road trip across California. Yosemite was the fourth stop on our eight-day trip and would be the place where we spent the majority of our time. I had dreamed of this. We had dreamed of this. For months on end, we had been sending stunning photos of Yosemite's sunrise in our group message, only adding to the already heightened anticipation. But now, the moment was finally here for us to experience it for ourselves.

I've loved photography since I was young. I've photographed sunrises on the East Coast, over Niagara Falls, over the Gulf Coast, and many other places. I've arrived to photograph a sunrise only to be met by a washed-out, gray sky. This time, more than ever, I was hoping the sky would be bursting with color.

All seven of us gathered our belongings out of the tent, loaded the car, and began our climb out of the valley. The day before, traffic had been so horrific that it took an hour to get through the valley. But this early in the morning, hardly anyone was on the road. As we began our climb, dawn had come, and the sky was changing from black to deep blue. At this point, there was enough light to see out the window of the Dodge Durango we were in. As we moved along, all we could see was gray, some of the densest fog I've ever seen. We had one shot at this, and I just knew it was going to be a dud.

We continued our ascent, but all I could see was fog. Fog, fog, more fog. Fog to my left, fog to my right, fog above me. We could hardly see the massive granite walls to our left and right. My heart began to sadden as I feared the dreaded gray sky would drown out any view of the sun bursting through the clouds right over Half Dome's majestic peak. As we continued to climb, I looked to my right, hoping to find any gap in the fog that would offer a glimpse of hope. With every minute, I noticed that the fog seemed to be less dense. We were almost to the top, and the anticipation was real. I was still holding on to hope until the very last minute. I looked to my right as we rounded the last corner that opened up into Tunnel View. I'll never forget that moment. My heart leapt, my eyes shot wide open, and my adrenaline began to pump as the fog I had seen the entire way up wasn't there. There was only minimal cloud cover, which meant there was a good chance that the sunrise was going to burst through with the iconic bright orange and pink hues.

We parked the car, and I grabbed my camera gear and darted over to the ledge to set up my tripod as I prepared for the sunrise I had always dreamed of photographing. When I reached the ledge, extended my tripod, and sat down, I gazed out over the valley, amazed at what I saw. El Capitan's 7,500-foot granite rock face was to my left, Bridal Veil Falls' aesthetic roar was to my right, and Half Dome's 8,800-foot perch peaked off in the distance. It was a spectacular sight. The moment was surreal. Beneath us was a low-hanging fog that blanketed itself between the granite walls and stretched across the entire valley as far as the eye could see. The white sheet gracefully formed around the valley's tallest trees, creating the most beautiful landscape I'd ever seen. It was only moments later that the sky began to change. The deep blue of the sky was met with a deep orange and red flare that stretched beyond Half Dome's peak, reflecting off the fog that continued to wisp over the valley floor. It was beautiful! I took many photos, but I also took the time to stand there and just gaze over the beauty of Yosemite.

The sun continued to climb over the valley, and I thought back to the drive up the mountain. When we first started, we couldn't see anything. Our view was totally obstructed by the dense fog around us. I realized something pivotal. If I had stayed on the valley floor to photograph the sunrise, I would have missed it. Even if I had driven 10 minutes to the other end of the valley, the fog would have still hindered me from seeing the beauty of this sunrise. I could have searched and searched for a way around it, but the only way of escape was up. Only from an elevated place was I able to see the beauty before me.

Here's what the Lord was teaching me.

In every moment of life, we *have* to see the way God sees. His perspective is always from above. Too often, we want the greater vision without making the journey to the higher place. We want to see the way He sees without seeing from the place He's seeing from. Because His perspective is from above, we must get to a higher place.

David wrote in one of his psalms:

> *For in the time of trouble*
> *He shall hide me in His pavilion;*
> *In the secret place of His tabernacle*
> *He shall hide me;*
> *He shall set me high upon a rock.*

And now my head shall be lifted up above my enemies
all around me.
Therefore, I will offer sacrifices of joy in His tabernacle;
I will sing, yes, I will sing praises to the LORD.

—Ps. 27:5–6

From an earthly perspective, it makes zero sense to praise the Lord in a time of trouble. The only reason David could sing praises and rejoice before the Lord in his time of trouble was because his perspective shifted, and he was not seeing from a worldly view. God had placed his feet upon the solid Rock. It was from that foundation that his eyes were positioned to see above what he once looked straight into. Standing on a higher, firmer, surer foundation, he was able to see above his adversary. *This* was a place of triumph. *This* was a place of victory. Therefore, he rejoiced.

The Father's desire is to place our feet upon that same Rock. It's not merely a physical rock as you may think, but rather it's the person of Jesus Christ—God's only begotten Son. As we stand upon the finished work of Jesus through the cross, we are *then* and *only then* positioned to see above what was once bigger than we are. It's *only* in that place that we stand in total victory.

This stance and this foundation don't come cheaply to anyone. In fact, let me rephrase that. It *didn't* come cheaply, but it was purchased at a ridiculously high price—too high for all of us combined to pay. But there was One who bought it. With His own blood, He entered the Most Holy Place and obtained eternal redemption (Heb. 9:12).

Just one verse before David's cry, he revealed the way to this foundation. If you don't remember anything else about this book, remember this:

One thing I have desired of the LORD,
That will I seek:
That I may dwell in the house of the LORD

All the days of my life,
To behold the beauty of the LORD,
And to inquire in His temple.

—Ps. 27:4

An elevated perspective doesn't begin in the eyes. It begins in one place—the heart. David's heart cry was inspiring to say the least. He didn't say "the first thing I have desired of the Lord." He said, "One thing I have desired of the Lord." In his heart, he only wanted one thing—to be with God every day of his life and to gaze upon His beauty and glory. It was out of this pure desire that He was placed upon that Rock, thus elevating his perspective and allowing him to see above what had come to trouble him.

For David, it all began with a quiet place. A secret place. A place behind a closed door, if you will. A meeting place with God. A place where intimacy developed and matured. Out of that place of intimacy, new perspective was birthed. Likewise for all of us, the route God chooses to reposition our perspective is through a place of intimacy with His Spirit. However, it's not just a repositioning of the eyes that the Lord is after. He is after the affection of our hearts.

You can spend your entire life trying to climb your way to the top of that Rock, but you'll never get there. It is not something that grit, determination, and muscular strength can attain. It is a place only attained through a posture of humility and worship because it's the humble who are exalted (1 Pet. 5). The Rock is the destiny of the humble, yielded heart devoted to seeking the face of Jesus. The way up is down—down on your knees, committed to a lifestyle of prayer, worship, and relationship with the Lord Jesus.

It's not an easy journey. In fact, it may be difficult, painful, and confusing at times. But God did promise us this: The rivers won't overflow us, the fire won't burn us, and the flame won't scorch us. Why? Because He's with us. So let Him take you on the journey He has so brilliantly and beautifully prepared for you. The calling on and purpose of your life is greater than you could ever dream. Take hold of His hand. Decide to embark today on a journey with the Lord. He will take you where He has called you.

On January 3, 2015, the Lord told me I wouldn't be moved because I was standing on the Rock. The journey wasn't easy. In fact, the rain hurt, the thunder was loud, and the lightning was scary at times. But here I stand today, upon the same Rock that has never broken. Upon the same foundation that's never collapsed. Upon that same Jesus whose faithfulness is unending. Forevermore, I'll stand upon this Rock with my hands lifted high in praise to my God. That's the place of victory.

My dad, Robby Edwards, shortly after he was diagnosed with cancer
(February 2015).

My family at our church in Rainbow City, Alabama
(December 2015).

Many of my dad's past players made a surprise visit to his house and honored him with a plaque for his many years of coaching (May 2016).

My family at our church in Rainbow City, Alabama (July 2016).

My dad reaching his goal of standing to preach (July 2016).

My family surrounded by our church family (July 2016).

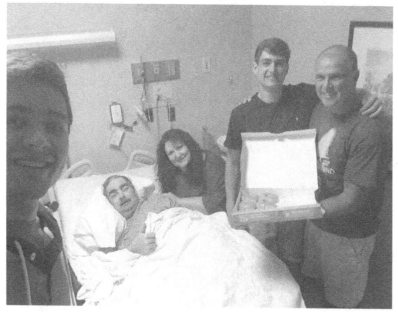

My family with Coach Pruitt on the day Dad was released from ICU and placed in a regular room (October 2016).

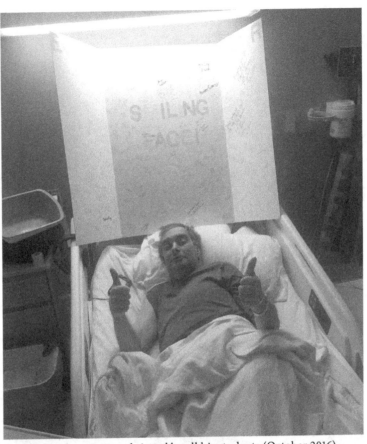

Dad with a giant card signed by all his students (October 2016).

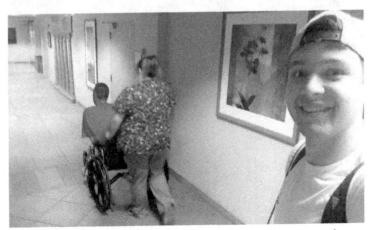

Dad leaving the hospital for the first time in more than two weeks.
(October 2016).

CPSIA information can be obtained
at www.ICGtesting.com
Printed in the USA
LVHW081003060220
646038LV00018BA/967

9 781632 964946